the UNEXPECTED JOURNEY

Other Books by Thom S. Rainer

the

UNEXPECTED
JOURNEY

CONVERSATIONS WITH PEOPLE

WHO TURNED FROM

OTHER BELIEFS TO

THOM S. RAINER

ZONDERVAN™

GRAND RAPIDS, MICHIGAN 49530 USA

We want to hear from you. Please send your comments about this book to us in care of zreview@zondervan.com. Thank you.

ZONDERVAN™

The Unexpected Journey
Copyright © 2005 by Thom S. Rainer

Requests for information should be addressed to:
Zondervan, *Grand Rapids, Michigan 49530*

Library of Congress Cataloging-in-Publication Data

Rainer, Thom S.
    The unexpected journey : conversations with people who turned from other beliefs to Jesus / Thom S. Rainer.
        p. cm.
    Includes bibliographical references and index.
    ISBN-10: 0-310-25741-7
    ISBN-13: 978-0-310-25741-7
        1. Christian converts—United States—Interviews.   I. Title.
BV4930.R35 2005
248.2'46'092273—dc22
                                                  2005013994

This edition printed on acid-free paper.

Interior design by Tracey Walker

Printed in the United States of America

05 06 07 08 09 10 /❖ DCI/ 10 9 8 7 6 5 4 3 2 1

To
Tom Hellams
Chuck Lawless
Brad Waggoner
Three great colleagues
Three great friends

And always to
Nellie Jo
Beauty. Courage. Love.

CONTENTS

ACKNOWLEDGMENTS

I remember well that chilly day in Grand Rapids as my wife, Nellie Jo, and I sat across the breakfast table from Paul Engle and Jim Ruark. Those two men have become more than editors of my books; they have become friends and encouragers. I was proposing a new book about people who have become Christians from other faiths. They not only said my idea was worthy of publication; their enthusiastic response made me believe that this book really could make a difference in many people's lives.

"Thank you" is simply not adequate for Paul, Jim, and Mike Cook, the ever-encouraging marketing guru at Zondervan. Indeed, words fail me to express gratitude for the entire Zondervan team. These men and women have become my friends and extended family.

In the twelve stories you are about to read, you will hear from thirteen extraordinary individuals. I am forever indebted to these six men and seven women. They gave me time. They gave me their testimonies. And they stole my heart in the process. Thank you, Rauni, Dennis, Steve, Ravi, Mrs. J., Paul, Mia, Kathi, Helena, Karan, Marsha, Mumin, and Jeff. I am convinced that your stories will be used by God to make an immeasurable impact on thousands of readers.

In the dedication you see the names of three men who work with me at the Southern Baptist Theological Seminary. I am grateful for great colleagues. But when these colleagues just happen to be three of my best friends, the blessings are multiplied. Tom, Brad, and Chuck are three of the most selfless and generous men I know. I will never take their friendships for granted.

As is the case with all my books, this book is also dedicated to my wife, Nellie Jo. My family is the greatest gift from God outside of my salvation through Jesus Christ. My sons, Art, Jess, and Sam, are incredible young men, and they encourage and advise me on all my books. But Nellie Jo's story is even more poignant.

My wife was an equal part of this entire *Unexpected Journey* project, and in many ways her name deserves to be on the cover as much as my own. She traveled with me all over the nation and asked better questions than I did. She established an immediate rapport with the thirteen people we interviewed and more than compensated for my socially dysfunctional personality. Further-more, she gave invaluable insights and suggestions. Yes, I wrote the pages of this book, but Nellie Jo is the coauthor of the project.

Nellie Jo was diagnosed with breast cancer just two weeks after the last interview. I have been amazed at her courage and selfless love as she travels the road of her own unexpected journey.

How can I express the love, devotion, and admiration I have for my wife? How can I say adequately how she has complemented and completed my life? Words are not sufficient. I do know that without her love and encouragement I wouldn't have written any books. And I also know that this book is more hers than mine in many respects.

Nellie Jo, you have heard and read it many times: I love you. I hope you have some idea of the depth and breadth of this love. I am with you every step of the way on your own difficult and unex-pected journey. And I have full confidence in God that we have many journeys left to travel in this great adventure called marriage and life.

PREFACE

BEFORE THE JOURNEY

My wife, Nellie Jo, and I started *The Unexpected Journey* interviews in Salt Lake City and ended them nearly a year later in Augusta, Georgia. The concept was simple. We wanted to hear from people who came from other belief systems to faith in Christ. We had no idea what to expect. What we both can say, however, is that these conversations were unlike any we had engaged in before. We heard stories of changed lives, and in the process we began to see our own lives changing as well.

Two of our interviews were conducted in the comfort of our hosts' homes. Several took place in restaurants, and a few of the conversations were in churches. In each case we heard stories that could best be described as miraculous. We heard stories of people on the brink of suicide discovering the life-giving and life-changing power of Jesus Christ. And we listened to some tell me how they learned to love and forgive after being consumed with bitterness and hate.

The path of this book is straightforward. I take you from city to city in the same order Nellie Jo and I traveled. For nine of the twelve interviews, my wife and I were the only researchers present. In three of the interviews, we had someone from our research team join us.

If you are a Christian reading this book, I pray that your faith will be strengthened. Such was the case for my wife and me. I also hope that you will learn to be bolder in sharing your faith. My wife said it best: "I simply don't have any hesitation sharing about Christ anymore. The interviews for *The Unexpected Journey* taught me that so many people truly desire to hear about Christ."

If you are not a Christian, allow me to share a few words with you. First, please understand that I approached this project from a clearly Christian bias. That will be plain as you proceed through the pages. But, second, know that I did my best to present each story as objectively as possible. I have attempted to avoid the "my faith is superior to yours" attitude that you probably experience too often from Christians. While I believe with every fiber of my being that Jesus Christ is the only way of salvation, I pray that my attitude throughout this project has been humble and transparent.

Before you begin, let me share with you what this book is *not*. First, it is not an apologetics book that provides extensive details on defending the Christian faith in a pluralistic world. I do believe the book has wide apologetic applications, but it is not specifically a book on apologetics.

Second, this book is not an exhaustive treatment of other belief systems. I provide sidebar information in each chapter that gives basic facts and figures about a particular belief. But much more comprehensive works on world religions and other beliefs are available.

This book is primarily the story of thirteen people from twelve non-Christian belief systems who became Christians. Most of the words in each chapter are direct quotes from the interview. My challenge was to condense dozens of hours of interviews into just a few pages.

My intention is to take you, the reader, on the journey with us. I hope you get a sense of the personalities of the people we interviewed. I hope you feel the intensity of their words and laugh at some of the humorous situations in which they found themselves. I hope you comprehend at least a portion of the pain so many of them endured, so that you can see the victories they have experienced.

Welcome to *The Unexpected Journey*. Prepare yourself for life-changing stories. Prepare to laugh. Prepare, perhaps, to shed a tear or two. And prepare to hear how God worked in some of the unlikeliest places.

Thank you for joining us. And as you read the stories of these changed lives, my prayer is that God will use this book to change your life for the better as well.

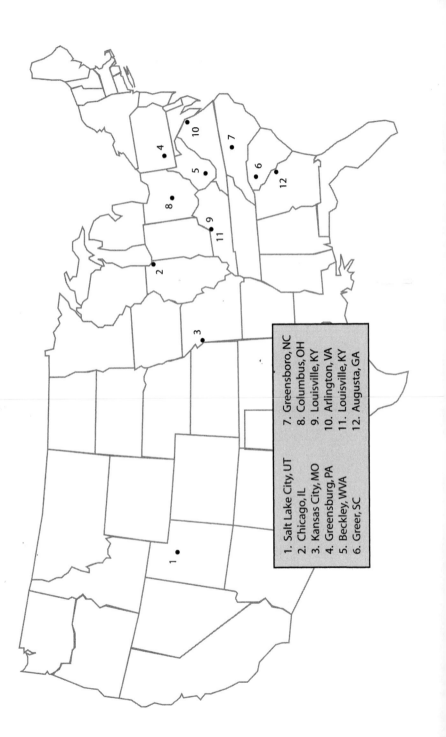

1. Salt Lake City, UT
2. Chicago, IL
3. Kansas City, MO
4. Greensburg, PA
5. Beckley, WVA
6. Greer, SC
7. Greensboro, NC
8. Columbus, OH
9. Louisville, KY
10. Arlington, VA
11. Louisville, KY
12. Augusta, GA

CHAPTER ONE

"MORMONISM WAS OUR LIFE"

AN INCREDIBLE JOURNEY TO CHRISTIANITY

April 12
Salt Lake City, Utah

My wife, Nellie Jo, and I boarded the plane leaving Louisville with mixed emotions. On the one hand, we still were not fully rested from our trip to Uganda that had ended just three days earlier. On the other hand, we were energized with anticipation of the interview that would soon take place. My research assistant, Stuart Swicegood, had worked very hard to find the people we would soon meet. A former Mormon couple, Dennis and Rauni Higley, would be waiting to tell us about their amazing pilgrimage from Mormonism to faith in Jesus Christ.

The connection in Atlanta went without a hitch. We arrived late at a hotel in downtown Salt Lake City, and sleep came quickly. In what seemed like the blink of an eye, we were getting ready the next morning to travel to the Higleys' home in a suburb of Salt Lake City.

A cloudless day with a bright blue sky greeted us as we left the hotel. We both breathed in the fresh air and felt the warmth of the mild spring day. If the weather was to be a sign of the hours ahead, the day would be good indeed.

My wife and I discussed our strategy for this interview—the first for this book—because we wanted to be ready for any contingency. I had a list of numerous questions I would be prepared to ask. Nellie Jo would keep the conversation going smoothly in the event that the discussion came to a lull.

The fifteen-minute drive to Sandy, Utah, was filled with constant conversation and the occasional interruption of the navigation computer in the rental car. I commented to Nellie Jo that every navigation system I used had a female voice, and I wondered why. My bride of twenty-seven years did not respond verbally, but her smile said it all.

As we pulled into the driveway of the Higley home, I looked at the mountains framing their home and neighborhood. The scene was postcard perfect.

A sign on the door of their home told us of a Finnish custom that asked all guests to remove their shoes. We rang the doorbell and were quickly greeted by a smiling couple.

Rauni Higley welcomed us with an accent that I did not recognize immediately. She would soon tell us that her native homeland was Finland. Her husband, Dennis, was a native of Idaho. Nellie Jo has a clear Alabama accent, and I have been told that I speak with a mix of midwestern twang and southern drawl. The interview recording of the four of us would prove to be a cacophony of voices!

Rauni's Story

Rauni and Dennis led us into their impeccably clean home, and we made ourselves comfortable. The digital recorder was set. After some introductory and casual conversation, I asked the first interview question: "Tell us about your background." I got the impression that Rauni could not wait to talk, so we all looked at her for the first response.

"I was born in Finland. My father died when I was eleven, and my mother died when I was seventeen. My grandparents had also passed away. I was an only child, so I was left with no family, just some aunts and uncles," she told us with a pause. We could tell that the years since their deaths had not removed all her pain.

Rauni continued, "I met a young lady who had joined the Mormon Church about a year earlier. She found out about all the deaths in my family, and she explained how my parents, grandparents, and I could be sealed together for eternity. She told me that through the Mormon Church I could get all my family back when this life is over."

> The official name of Mormonism is the Church of Jesus Christ of Latter-day Saints. With 12 million members and more than 300,000 converts a year, this movement is among the fastest-growing in the world. Mormons are also one of the wealthiest religious groups in the world, with assets estimated at between 25 and 30 billion dollars.

There was little need to persuade Rauni further. "I didn't have any spiritual foundations," she told us. "They told me that everyone who had not heard the Mormon gospel would get a second chance after death. The names of my parents and grandparents could be taken to the temple, and they could be baptized. It all sounded so great to me."

Mormons became Rauni's family as she joined their church in 1963. "I met with a small group in an apartment. It was a really nice and friendly group of people. We all called each other 'brother and sister.' I never had a brother or sister, and I had no family," she explained.

Rauni became an enthusiastic Mormon. "I read everything in Finland published by the Mormon Church. I read the *Book of Mormon* right away. I didn't detect any errors in it because I was not that familiar with the Bible. So it sounded just like the Bible to me."

I wish everyone could meet Rauni. As we sat in her family room that day, Nellie Jo and I were mesmerized by her enthusiasm. She spoke with excitement and sparkling eyes. We could easily see how that same enthusiasm could have been directed toward her new religion.

"The mission president in Helsinki heard I was excited about being a new convert," she affirmed. "He came to visit me even though I had been a member for only nine months. He told me that the president of the Mormon Church, David O. McKay, had called me to be a missionary for the church in Finland. I was so impressed. The prophet of God of the Mormon Church had called me to be a missionary!"

Rauni would serve two years as a missionary gladly. But she knew what her next goal would be. "I wanted to be where everybody is a Mormon; that's my family," she recalled. "So I moved to Salt Lake City and started working for the Mormon Church as a translator and interpreter. The church had just started a translation department, but the only translators were Spanish translators. I was hired to translate English to Finnish."

Dennis Responds

Nellie Jo was curious about another issue. How did Dennis and Rauni meet? To this point Dennis had remained quiet. But you could see the love and pride in his eyes as Rauni told her story. We asked him to answer the question.

"I was a sixth-generation Mormon," Dennis told us. "The Mormon Church had always been my life, and I knew nothing else. I was serving as a missionary to Finland for two and a half years. I met Rauni there. When she moved to Salt Lake City, we started courting seriously and, of course, eventually got married in the Salt Lake Mormon Temple."

Dennis continued, "My family was very active in the church, and I never thought about any life outside the church. And when I met Rauni and married her, we wanted to be the perfect Mormon couple. I had a long history and heritage in the church, and I would rise quickly to leadership positions in my ward and stake. [A stake is a Mormon territorial jurisdiction comprising a group of wards.] And Rauni was working in the middle of all the action at the Salt Lake City headquarters."

Nellie Jo and I had traveled across country to hear how two devout Mormons had become Christians. I tried to be patient as I heard their backgrounds, but I was grateful when my wife asked the question straightforwardly: "So what made the two of you leave Mormonism?" We couldn't wait to hear the response, and Rauni was more than happy to tell us that story.

"Mormonism Just Doesn't Make Sense"

"I ended up working in the translation department of the Mormon Church for over fourteen years," Rauni began. "Translation involves a lot of research. The church is always trying to prove that Mormonism is unchanging from Joseph Smith's time to this day."

> In 1823 Joseph Smith claimed to receive a revelation from God that all churches were corrupt. He said that the angel Moroni appeared to him in upstate New York and revealed to him the location of gold plates that contained the history of God's people on this American continent and the fullness of the true gospel. Mormonism began with teachings of the Book of Mormon that Smith claimed he had "translated" from the Reformed Egyptian hieroglyphic characters on the plates.

Rauni continued to explain her work for the Mormon Church. "Most of the literature I was assigned to translate had quotes from different Mormon prophets, such as Joseph Smith, Brigham Young, and others. Even though the quotes were generally only small paragraphs, I wanted to read them from their original texts to make sure I understood the context clearly.

"The longer I worked and the more I translated, the more I could see that Mormon teachings contradict themselves, depending upon who is the prophet at the time," Rauni explained with intensity. "For example, I saw where Brigham Young taught for twenty-five years that Adam was actually God and the father of Jesus. But the Mormon Church does not teach that today. Each of these prophets were said to be spokesmen for God, but they all disagreed with each other on many important points."

I interjected, "Did you immediately start rejecting Mormonism when you saw these contradictions?"

This time Rauni spoke slowly. "It really took me many years to believe what I was seeing with my own eyes. When you believe in something so strongly for so many years, you doubt your own ability to evaluate things. I was thinking that there must be something wrong with me, not the church."

Eventually Rauni finally could not doubt the massive number of contradictions she read and translated. The evidence was just too overwhelming. "Mormonism just doesn't make sense," she told us. By 1981 she could no longer keep the troubling conflict to herself. She had to show her husband all she had learned in her fourteen years as a translator.

A Pause and a Perspective

When I listened to the recording of the interview several weeks later, I heard sniffles at this point. There were several emotional moments during the interview, but I couldn't quite discern who was crying at this juncture. Then I heard my own voice: "Folks, I need a break. My nose is running like crazy!" Leave it to me and my allergies to interrupt a poignant and critical moment in the interview.

But the unplanned pause was beneficial. The interview had been very intense to this point. We all really needed time to breathe and take a break. The short recess also offered me a perspective on what had been said.

Nellie Jo and I were not merely interviewing two "typical" former Mormons. We were hearing from a sixth-generation Mormon and a Mormon who for fourteen years had access to some of the most important and secretive documents in the church. Their defection from the Mormon Church had to have presented a serious threat to their former associates. I was right, but I never would have imagined the incredible price the Higleys would have to pay. We will hear more on that issue shortly. For now, let's hear from Rauni and Dennis what happened as they began to study the Mormon contradictions together.

"From Mormonism to Nothingism"

"When Rauni could no longer keep her discoveries to herself," Dennis explained, "she began to show me contradiction after contradiction in some of the most important Mormon teachings. We went into an intense study of Mormon history and doctrine, things I had been taught since I was a child. The more we dug, the more we found out it was not true. We finally came to the conclusion that Mormonism is based on fraud and deception. We discovered that it was simply a fraudulent man-made organization and that we had to separate ourselves from it."

> *Joseph Smith claimed that the Book of Mormon was the most perfect and complete book on earth. He and Mormons today believe that all translations of the Bible are corrupt. He first published the Book of Mormon in 1830. Smith founded the movement in New York State and moved it to Ohio and then to Missouri because of opposition. After Smith was murdered in Illinois in 1844, Brigham Young took over the leadership and relocated the group to Utah.*

Decision time came in 1983 for Dennis and Rauni. They sent a letter to the Mormon Church requesting that their names be removed from the membership rolls. Dennis told us that he also made the decision that he would never have anything to do with any religion again. "My decision was to move from Mormonism to nothingism. I was angry, particularly at the Mormon Church, but I also had begun to distrust all religions in general."

A Difficult Decision

My wife asked the insightful question, "Did you get any kind of negative feedback from the church?"

We could still feel the emotions of many years earlier as Dennis responded. "We had lots of trouble. I was in a leadership position in the church. I was on the Stake High Council, one of twelve men who, with the stake presidency, preside over several wards or congregations. I had been promoted to this position based upon my activity and faithfulness to the church. And Rauni was involved in high positions in the church women's organization in addition to her translation work."

Rauni then added, "You have to understand how tough this decision was for us. Dennis was a sixth-generation Mormon. And I realized that if Mormonism was not true, then I would not get to see my family again." Rauni paused. She recalled that moment with tears in her eyes. She explained softly, "I so much wanted to hang on to that hope."

Dennis admitted that he was reluctant to leave Mormonism. "Rauni had been questioning some things for some time because of her research. But I was not ready at first to hear her arguments."

Rauni interjected, "I had just read a book exposing Mormonism by former Mormons. I thought if I could get Dennis to read that book, he would have the testimony of someone else, not just me."

"Rauni challenged me," Dennis said with a smile and a twinkle in his eyes. "I accused the author of that book of being anti-Mormon, a buzzword among Mormons for anyone who speaks against their church. Finally, she challenged me to test the book with all the Mormon books we had and to expose the authors as being anti-Mormon. I finally took her up on it. I was ready to expose them."

> Mormons believe that all people will eventually be resurrected and get into one of three heavenly kingdoms. But only Mormons who have faithfully followed the teachings of the church will enter the highest heaven, which they call the celestial kingdom. They also teach that God was once a mortal man and that men can become gods.

Nellie Jo acknowledged Rauni's resolve, exclaiming, "You are one determined lady!" Dennis and I looked at each other and smiled as we recognized that the two women had already developed an affinity for each other.

Dennis continued, "So we sat down at the table with a stack of Mormon books and started to compare what the anti-Mormons had written. I was determined to expose them! Rauni began giving me quotes from this book, and I would look them up in the Mormon books. We stayed up until 2:00 a.m., and everything in the anti-Mormon book proved true."

Nellie Jo smiled knowingly. "Were you angry?"

We could almost hear Dennis grinding his teeth. "Was I angry? I was so angry! I had given the Mormon Church my life. I had followed their teachings without question. I had done everything they asked. But I started to see everything was based on lies. I had been deceived. I was really, really angry!"

Dennis would not sleep well that night. "I slammed all the books shut. 'That's enough,' I said. I took my Sunday school manual back to the church the next Sunday and told them I would never be back. I was just livid!"

From Nothingness to Faith in Christ

"So for the next year and a half," Dennis said more calmly now, "Sunday became a day off. I knew in my heart there had to be a

God, but I wanted nothing to do with religions. Once burned, twice smart. I decided not to ever have anything to do with any religion ever again."

But God had other plans.

The Higleys were successful businesspersons. They owned a thriving retail business and were successful real estate developers. One of the employees in the Higleys' retail store, not knowing of their break with the Mormon Church, asked Rauni what church position she now had.

"I told her that I didn't go to church any longer," Rauni said. I said, 'I don't have anything to do with it.' So one day she showed up at my home and asked if I would listen to three Bible study tapes. The tapes were a commentary on the Gospel of John. I was annoyed with her request, but she was so nice that I promised her I would listen to them."

Two weeks would pass before Rauni thought about the tapes. "Then I remembered them and my promise. I thought I could just turn them on while cleaning and cooking. But as the tape played, I had to stop my work. I was drawn to every word the man on the tape said. I got my Bible and a notebook. I listened and took notes until the last tape played."

The Christian employee, Linda, had made a difference with a simple act. "I was so excited!" Rauni exclaimed. "There is truth! Now I know who Jesus really is!"

> Mormons believe that Jesus is not God, but the eldest of all spirit children of God and his many wives. They also believe that Jesus and Lucifer are spirit brothers and brothers of all mankind and angels because they were procreated by the same parents.

"The three tapes Linda gave me covered only the first few verses in the Gospel of John," Rauni told us. "I called her and asked her if I could have the rest of the tapes. But she told me that those were the only ones she had. So I called the company whose name was on the tape and got the complete set of twenty-two tapes."

By this point in the interview, we had no doubt that Rauni was indeed one determined woman. "Yep," Dennis said with a smile. "She listened to all twenty-two tapes in no time. Yep, she started asking me to listen to the tapes. I told her no. She then begged me to listen to just the first tape and promised she wouldn't bug me anymore. I finally gave in."

I looked at Dennis and told him I understood completely.

Dennis may have lost the battle, but he would still show his stubbornness. "I sat down to listen to the first tape, and I literally turned my back to the recorder. The man on the tape then began to explain John 1:1. For forty-five minutes he explained one verse and who Jesus is. Who the 'Word' is.

"Forty years of my life, and I had never heard this explained." Dennis paused. The moment was one of deep emotion. "There it was. This was incredible. I turned the chair around and asked Rauni, 'What's on the second one?' I started taking notes, writing in my Bible for the first time. We finished the second tape."

Dennis explained his next step. "I told Rauni we ought to start the study over with our daughters. For the next year and a half, we studied the Bible together on Sunday as a family. It was incredible."

"How did your daughters respond?" Nellie Jo asked.

"They were all very open, very receptive. Now all three of them are Christians." Dennis beamed.

"All of this was so very incredible," Rauni offered. "I realized that I had found through the Gospel of John that Jesus is God; he is God with us; he really is God." Rauni was no longer able to hold her tears. "I finally just fell down on my face," she said, weeping. "I said, 'Lord, come into my life, take over my life.' I was so convicted that Jesus is God, not my brother as the Mormon Church teaches."

Several months would pass before Dennis accepted Christ. "While doing Bible study, I was also digging into Mormonism more deeply. I read all about the history of Mormonism. I too fell flat on my face one day and accepted Jesus as my Savior," he told us. That moment of recall was deeply emotional. Dennis choked a bit and said, "For forty years I had been following a false god. And now I found the one true God."

Finding a Church Home

For several more months, the Higleys studied the Bible in their home, until their studies led them to the conclusion that they would have to be baptized and affiliate with a local church. The process of finding a church was not easy. Utah is dominated by the Mormon Church.

> The Mormon Church claims to be the one true church with the only true beliefs. One of their beliefs, among many, that contradict Christian doctrine is their denial of the Trinity, that God is one God in three persons. Mormons believe that the Father, the Son, and the Holy Spirit are three separate Gods.

Eventually the Higleys found a church home, a Baptist church of some seventy-five members. When Dennis told the pastor that he would never again have anything to do with Mormonism, the pastor countered by saying that perhaps God had given him a great opportunity to equip others to reach Mormons for Christ.

"So I started teaching a Sunday evening class on how to reach Mormons," Dennis sighed. "Before we knew it, our class was packed. People really wanted to know how to reach their Mormon friends and neighbors."

"What did you teach them?" I asked.

"Really, we just taught two basic issues," Dennis responded. "First, Christians must know their Bible. Mormons devour Christians who don't study their Bibles. Second, Christians need to ask

Mormons questions. Most of the time when a Mormon shows up at a Christian's home, the Christian immediately begins to talk about his beliefs. But the Mormon has been trained to say, 'Oh, we believe that too.' Mormons use the same words as Christians, but the meanings are really different."

Dennis continued, "You have to get the Mormons to talk about their God, Jesus, and salvation first, and then show them their errors by the Bible."

The story of this Utah Baptist church is amazing. As more and more of the members grew in confidence in sharing their faith with their Mormon neighbors, the church began to grow. Within a year the church had more than doubled to two hundred members. It was not much longer before the membership level reached five hundred.

"It was an incredible time," Rauni exclaimed. "Mormons were accepting Christ almost every week. I remember one huge man—"

"That man was six feet six inches tall and weighed over 250 pounds," Dennis interjected.

Rauni continued, "He came running down the aisle to tell the pastor he wanted to accept Christ. He had big tears falling down on his face. God was really doing a work."

A Time of Trouble

The time with the Higleys had gone too quickly. I still had one big missing piece of information for the interview. Dennis and Rauni had mentioned some difficult days after they left the Mormon Church. Nellie Jo and I waited to hear that story

"After we sent our letter asking the Mormon Church to remove our names from their records," Dennis began, "they held an excommunication court. The bishop announced to the church that we had been excommunicated. He gave no reason for the excommunication, and the rumors began to fly. Everyone assumed I had committed adultery. By the end of the week, the rumor was that I was a polygamist with six or seven wives."

Dennis would not stand still. "I started telling people why we had left the church. I told them that we had studied the Bible and compared Mormon teachings for months, and we saw clearly that Mormonism is based on deception and is not of God and the Bible."

The Higleys became a threat to the Mormon Church. The members knew that both Dennis and Rauni were no novices in the church. Their words had too many notes of credibility that rang true. The Mormon leadership decided to respond.

"They decided to make an example of us," Dennis remembered. "In their quarterly stake conference, they announced that no one should do business with the Higleys since they had left the church."

Rauni added, "They forbade anyone from having business dealings with us."

The Mormon strategy worked.

"It was a tough time," Rauni recalled. "While we were bringing dozens of Mormons to Christ, our businesses were being ruined. We were pretty well-to-do, but both our retail and real estate businesses were suffering. We started taking out loans, thinking that this would blow over. It didn't."

The Higleys would ultimately have to liquidate all their assets. Financial advisors urged them to declare bankruptcy so they could avoid paying some of their debt, but the Higleys refused. They were Christians now; they did not want their testimony harmed. Even after all the assets were sold, Dennis and Rauni had a sizable debt to repay.

"It took us about ten years to pay off everyone, but we did," Rauni said with a smile. "Everybody got their money back. I am so thankful we went through this. It taught us how little material and worldly things really matter."

Dennis concurred, "It cost us a lot. We lost everything materially, but in the end we got the prize. We got Jesus Christ."

I left the Higley home with a lump in my throat. Nellie Jo and I were quiet as we got in the car and headed back to the Salt Lake City airport. Although the Higleys have partially recovered from their financial disaster, they are not nearly as affluent as they once were. But they don't care. They have found something far greater than money. They have found Jesus. And they know everything else pales in comparison.

The mountain air of Utah was even fresher than when we first arrived. The sky was bluer, and our spirits were soaring. We had been witnesses to the testimony of a miracle. This time I really was not anxious to return to Louisville. My heart was still in the warm and friendly home of Dennis and Rauni Higley. Christ had changed their lives, and I had been impacted powerfully by their story.

The flight would connect in Cincinnati before taking us home to Louisville. Looking out the airplane window on the long trip back, I wondered if we would ever hear a story as powerful and moving as the one we had just heard. God would be good to us, and we ultimately would hear twelve amazing stories.

The next several days would be spent catching up at the seminary, speaking in other places, and teaching in the classroom. But in twenty short days, Nellie Jo and I would be sitting in a Chicago restaurant listening to the moving testimony of a vivacious messianic Jew named Steve. To his story we now turn.

CHAPTER TWO

"I HAVE FOUND THE MESSIAH!"

A JEW DISCOVERS HIS SAVIOR

April 30
Chicago, Illinois

In contrast to the beautiful and worry-free journey to Salt Lake City, the trip to Chicago was initially ugly and worry-filled. On the way from the Chicago O'Hare airport to our interview, I drove in a heavy thunderstorm and missed a turn in the city that made me late for my appointment. On the return trip I lost my driver's license at the airport and could not fly home because I did not have photo identification. My wife rented a car and drove us home to Louisville.

But that is the bad part. The rest of the story is an amazing blessing.

Our appointment was with Steve Barack, a Jew who worships Jesus as his Messiah. After we called Steve to let him know we were lost somewhere in the outer realms of Chicago, he guided us to the restaurant where we were scheduled to meet. I played the part of the dutiful gentlemen and let Nellie Jo and Deborah Morton, one of our researchers, get out at the restaurant door. I parked in the hinterlands and arrived soaked and doubting my sanity for a brief moment.

The early evening hours and cloud-filled skies produced a gloomy darkness that was not typical of this late April date. But once I walked in the restaurant, my momentary gloom dissipated. The restaurant was alive with noise and friendly chattering. I would soon learn that I was in a multigenerational Greek family establishment that catered to its surrounding Jewish population and was always friendly and busy.

Nellie Jo and Deborah had already been greeted by Steve Barack. My somewhat reserved personality was no match for this vivacious Jew who greeted me as a long-lost brother. I attempted to thank Steve for the time he was giving us, but he kept expressing his gratitude to me for the opportunity.

We sat down at the table to look at the menu. My wife saw the look of panic on my face. After nearly three decades of marriage, she understands my picky eating habits. I tend to focus on three food groups: meat, potatoes, and diet soda. The Greek-styled Jewish foods did not seem promising, but Nellie Jo had already found a plain dish. "You can eat this," she assured me.

The recorder was turned on, but the adventure had already begun.

Three Mandates

I was supposed to begin the interview, but I am not sure if any of us really did much questioning. Steve began without prompting. "Guys, I live by three mandates. We must love God with every part of our being. Second, we must love our neighbor with equal intensity. And finally, we must take the gospel of Jesus to anyone and everyone without any hesitation."

The waitress brought our orders to the table. We were in Chicago, but she seemed to speak with a Brooklyn accent, "Who has the BLT?" Hers was the best heard voice on the recorder.

Somehow we were able to get Steve to regress. One of our primary purposes was to hear his story. Our new friend came from multiple generations of Orthodox Jews. And while he insists that he has not lost one bit of his "Jewishness," he does believe that Jesus is the Son of God, that he is the Messiah, the fulfillment of the Jewish prophecies. We wanted to hear his story from the beginning. We would soon forget about the gloomy conditions outside as we heard this man's story and witnessed the joy of Christ radiating from his life.

An Unlikely Candidate to Become a Disciple of Christ

"I am always hesitant to give my testimony," Steve insisted. "I really want the focus to be on the Lord." But he realized that the purpose of our trip to Chicago was to hear his story, so he began a powerful testimony of the unrelenting love of God.

"I was raised in an Orthodox Jewish home that goes back as many generations as you can imagine," he began. "My family includes Orthodox Jews and Orthodox Jewish rabbis. My family came to America in 1925. Before that, their home was very similar to what you see when you watch *Fiddler on the Roof.*" Steve was referring to the story set in the small Jewish village of Anatevka, Russia, in 1904. The primary character is Tevye the milkman, a Jewish peasant coping with the day-to-day problems of his family, his Jewish traditions, and state-sanctioned pogroms.

> *Three major divisions exist in Judaism:*
>
> - *Orthodox Judaism is the oldest and most conservative branch. Orthodox Jews strictly adhere to the original form of Judaism with all of its customs and practices.*
> - *Reform Judaism is the liberal and more permissive side of Judaism. Reform Jews follow the ethical laws of Judaism but ignore other traditional customs such as diet and apparel.*
> - *Conservative Judaism is a compromise between the strict adherence of the Orthodox position and the permissive stance of the Reform perspective.*

"My father was the youngest and worldliest of my grandfather's four sons," Steve continued. "He did not raise me as strictly as my cousins were raised. Still, at eight years old, I was sent to attend a very intense Hebrew school. My high school was a yeshiva, a pre-rabbinate parochial school that I attended from 7:30 in the morning to 9:00 at night, six days a week."

The waitress announced in her not-so-demure voice that tea and soda refills were on the way. That gave Nellie Jo an opportunity to ask Steve if Jesus was ever a consideration in his family.

"Christ never came up," he responded quickly. "You see, we were very wary of all Gentiles. Jews were turned back by Americans and Europeans to die in the death camps of the Holocaust. We were routinely discriminated against. I was beat up a number of times as a young man."

His voice softened for a moment. "From our Jewish perspective, everyone else is a Christian. So if an atrocity happens to a Jew, they say a Christian did it. Many Jews even think of Hitler as a Christian."

Steve paused a moment and then continued. "So from many Jews' perspective, you can be a secular Jew, a Jew who is a Buddhist, or a New Age Jew worshiping trees and stones. But the moment you mention Christ, you're not a Jew. I was really an unlikely candidate to become a Christian."

> If there is one overarching doctrinal truth of Judaism, it takes the form of the Shema, which faithful Jews are to recite twice daily: "Hear, O Israel: The LORD is our God, the LORD is one." Moses records this in Deuteronomy 6:4.

"I Just Ran Away"

For several moments Steve talked about the westernization of Christianity. He is passionate about the need to restore the faith to its historical roots instead of adopting much of the pagan culture.

Still, our purpose was to hear his story, so my wife resumed her role as the verbal traffic cop. She directed Steve back to his story. "What happened after you finished school?" she asked.

Nellie Jo, Deborah, and I all noticed a change in Steve's demeanor. This part of the story was obviously painful.

"I just ran away," Steve enunciated slowly. "I was so confused. There was so much conflict and confusion in my beliefs and my attitude toward my family. For years I had been trained and educated in the best of Jewish schools. I knew the laws and the traditions. But I did not see consistency in those beliefs at home. All that I was taught to believe, my whole identity, just did not have consistency, so I bolted. I just ran away."

I attempted to bring some levity to this moment of deep introspection. Not recognizing the food on his plate, I asked, "What is that stuff you're eating?"

Steve responded, "Fried matzah, unleavened bread with eggs," he noted.

"Oh," I replied with feigned enthusiasm.

"I came to faith in Christ twenty years ago," he said, stirring his food but not eating. "My parents have nothing to do with me. My sister is a feminist Orthodox Jew; she has nothing to do with me. But I wouldn't trade my spot in life for anything in the world."

We were all eager to hear the story of the time Steve became a Christian two decades earlier. He would lead us to that point.

A Blonde Hairstylist and a Charismatic Pastor

"After I left home," he began, "I took a job in an automobile dealership in Chicago as a salesman. I was a gifted salesman, so I rose through the ranks quickly. I was soon the general manager, making good money. I was trying hard to distance myself from the Jewish teachings of my youth. I found myself out on the street partying every night and getting involved in multiple dating relationships."

Steve continued his story. "During this time in the 1970s I started going to a certain hairstylist, a cute blonde, and we started dating. We dated off and on for six or seven years, but she left the hairstylist shop to start her own place. So we both kind of forgot about each other for a while."

> *Judaism was the first of the major religions to believe in one God. The religion begins with Abraham, who was given three great promises, or covenants.*
>
> * *The first promise was that the Jews would be the people of God through whom others would learn about the one true God (Genesis 12:3).*
> * *The second promise was that Abraham would be the father of a great nation (Genesis 15:5).*
> * *The third promise to Abraham was that of a homeland for him and his descendants (Genesis 17:8).*

But Steve could still find no joy in his life. The partying continued and the hopelessness in his heart became an unfilled void. "I lived on the fifth floor of this nice apartment building overlooking Lake Michigan. Several times I seriously contemplated jumping off my balcony and ending all my pain there."

But God had other plans.

Steve never in our interview indicated that the Jewish beliefs he had learned so well as a young person were false. Unlike all the other interviews in this book, Steve did not convert away from his beliefs. He would ultimately learn that Christ was the fulfillment of his Judaism. How that came to take place is the fascinating rest of his story.

The cute hairstylist, Maureen, had strayed from her Christian faith for several years. But when she left to start her own shop, she did hairstyling and makeup for a Christian model. That model's testimony to Maureen helped the young hairstylist recommit her life to Christ.

Maureen eventually returned to the place where she had originally met Steve. He recalls that moment. "She asked me how I was doing. I told her that I guessed I was searching for my spirituality. Life had become such a void for me. I had no substance. I only had an unhealthy fear of God. I literally felt nothing. I was dead on the inside. Physically, I hardly ate anything. I was down to 130 pounds."

Maureen was attending an Assembly of God. Steve noted, "She was on fire for the Lord, and she saw me as a project. When I told her I was searching for my spirituality, she locked and loaded!"

> There are approximately 18 million Jews throughout the world. The largest numbers of Jews, about 7 million, are in the United States. The next largest concentration is in Israel, about 5 million.

Steve asked Maureen for a date. She would go out with him but to lunch only. "I said, 'No other time?' and she said, 'Yeah, Sunday mornings.' I asked where, and she said church. I told her I didn't do church. So we compromised, and I started picking her up after church."

Maureen was not satisfied with this arrangement. She told Steve that they couldn't continue dating if he didn't come to church.

Steve began attending the Assembly of God. After one service the pastor asked him what he thought about it. Steve responded, "Nice music."

The pastor then asked forthrightly, "What about Jesus?" Steve just laughed and didn't answer. What could he possibly know about Jesus?

"As much as I was running away from my Jewishness, I was still a Jew. And I saw going to a Christian church to be a complete abandonment of who I was," Steve told us.

Maureen recognized the struggle Steve was experiencing, so she convinced him to see her pastor.

"Actually, I went to see the pastor just to placate her," Steve clarified. "At this point I had nothing to lose. Little did I know how a cute blonde and a charismatic pastor were about to change my life radically."

A Jew Meets His Messiah

Before Steve continued, Deborah asked him if anyone had shared with him about Christ other than the cute blonde and her charismatic friends.

"No one," Steve replied. "I dated a lot of girls who said they were Christians or that they went to church, but that was about it. If I had Christian coworkers, I never would have known it. It is absolutely amazing how few Christians are willing and eager to share the gospel."

We returned to the story of Steve's encounter with the Assembly of God pastor. "He had his Bible open," Steve recalls. "Of course, I knew the Old Testament part better than he did. We went back and forth arguing. Neither one of us was getting anywhere. In a moment of exasperation, the pastor exclaimed, 'Steve, don't you know that God loves you?' It was like I heard an audible voice of God telling me to shut up and believe."

That was the breaking point for Steve. "For the first time, I let him present the gospel. For the first time, I just listened."

Steve now was beginning to understand. His Jewish faith did not have to be repudiated. Instead, the New Testament showed that Jesus Christ was the fulfillment of all the Jewish hope and prophecies about a coming Messiah.

> The early Christian church was comprised primarily of Jews who believed that Jesus was the Messiah. But other Jews did not believe that he was. This strong anti-Jesus sentiment born in Judaism has resulted historically in persecution against the Jews.

"The pastor took me home, but I could not say a word. I guess he knew that the Holy Spirit was convicting me, so he remained quiet as well," Steve recalled. "I went home and did not leave for three days. I cried almost the whole time. When the three days were over, I came to faith. I believed in Christ."

The atmosphere at the restaurant table was intense. We all seemed to welcome the interruption from the Brooklyn-accented Chicago waitress in the multigenerational Greek restaurant. "Can I get the table cleared, Honey?" she seemed to say to none of us in particular. We assured her that her presence was fine.

The break was expanded when Maureen called Steve on his cell phone. We waited a moment after he concluded talking to her, and then he resumed his story.

"For three days," Steve said in a more subdued voice, "I just cried and thought about the fact that God loved me. It all began to make sense. I found the Messiah. But it took a young and inexperienced charismatic pastor to say those powerful words, 'God loves you.'"

Steve did not go to work during that three-day period. When he returned, he was met in his office by a coworker. The fellow employee looked at Steve and said, "You've placed your faith in Christ, haven't you?"

Steve looked at him with incredulity and nodded.

"Good," said the coworker, "I can now resign my job."

Steve was not certain that he had heard the man correctly. "Did you say you are quitting your job?" Steve asked.

The fellow employee replied calmly, "Yes, the only reason I stayed at this place of work was to pray for you and to witness to you. Now that you are a Christian, I can move on. My purpose here has been fulfilled."

The man's name was Fred Hoff. He continued to pray for Steve and to be his friend. Fred died of brain cancer two years ago at the age of forty-two. "He left behind a beautiful wife and five gorgeous kids," Steve said wistfully. Prior to his death, Fred preached in the church where Steve now serves.

"Many people started coming out of the woodwork and telling me they were praying for me to become a Christian," Steve recounts.

He can see clearly the hand of God working through people and circumstances.

> *One of the primary sources of authority for Jews is the written Torah, also called the Tanakh. The Tanakh contains the same thirty-nine books that Christians know as the Old Testament. The books are arranged in different order in the Tanakh. The first five books are "the Law," or the books of Moses. The other thirty-four books are known as "the Prophets" and "the Writings."*

Christian but Still a Jew

After Steve became a believer in Christ, his courtship with Maureen accelerated. They soon married and were blessed with the adoption of a baby daughter. They also started looking for a church home where they both would feel comfortable. For Steve, none of the churches seemed to be a fit. The problem, Steve realized, was not the churches as much as himself.

Steve had discovered not a new faith but the fulfillment of his Jewish faith. He felt like he was more a Jew now than at any point in his life. But the churches he and his wife visited did not connect with his Jewish heritage.

"We were given some tapes of messianic Jewish music," Steve told us. "When we started playing them, our one-year-old daughter started clapping and jumping. We had never seen her do that with any other music we played."

He continued. "At the same time, I was really trying to figure out my new identity. My Jewish family rejected me, and most Christians had trouble understanding me. But when we played the messianic Jewish music, I knew who I was. I was a Jew who believed that Jesus was my Messiah.

"My wife and I started going to messianic congregations," he continued. "She is really a saint. She puts up with me, and she has become as Jewish as I am. But when we started going to the messianic congregations, we felt like we were home. The culture and the identity are Jewish, but we all worship Jesus Christ as our Messiah and God. It all makes sense now."

Steve's job, however, often interfered with his attendance at the messianic churches. "I was still working in the car business, and Saturday was one of our busiest days. But most of the messianic congregations have services on Saturday," he recalled.

Steve remained as active as he could with his work schedule. He was asked to teach youth, and in 1996 he started teaching adults. Shortly thereafter Steve started preaching and became a regular in the pulpit ministry. God opened the door even wider in the spring of 1999 when Steve was approached by the Southern Baptist Convention to plant a church in Chicago. With that offer, he was able to give full-time attention to his calling of leading a messianic congregation.

> *Orthodox Jews believe that God explained the meaning of the written Torah to Moses. Moses has since passed these teachings on to other people. These teachings were eventually transcribed in a book called the Mishnah. Additional commentaries, called the Gemera, were written over the next few centuries to expand on the Mishnah. The Gemera and Mishnah together are called the Talmud.*

Although he had to return to bivocational status two years later, Steve continues to lead the congregation called B'nai Ohr Beth Tefilah. The congregation meets in the Chicago suburb of Lindenhurst. Steve showed us the congregation's statement of faith and purpose.

B'nai Ohr Beth Tefilah is a house of worship where all people can come to worship together. In the Torah, the five books of Moses, G-d promised to deliver a Redeemer to Israel who would fulfill his covenant with Abraham, Isaac, and Jacob, and bless all nations by breaking down the wall of division between Jews and Gentiles. The prophetic scriptures throughout the Tanach/Hebrew Bible all point to Yeshua HaMashiakh (Jesus the Messiah) as that Redeemer.

We at B'nai Ohr celebrate the Shabbat on Saturday with a blend of contemporary and traditional music, Davidic dancing, hand clapping and prayer, incorporating some of the traditional Jewish/Biblical liturgy. This includes a Torah procession and blessing of children along with many traditional prayers.

Nellie Jo, Deborah, and I attended the service the next day, a Saturday with a bit of sunshine. I was honored to participate in the Scripture reading and the blessing of the children. Please be assured that I did not dance.

From Nothing to Evangelist

Steve Barack had told us of an incredible and unexpected journey. From Orthodox Judaism to nothing, to messianic Jew, to an evangelist of the gospel of Jesus Christ—he never could have predicted or planned this path. But you could not be around Steve for any length of time and not catch his contagious enthusiasm. He simply cannot understand why all Christians do not have that overflowing desire to tell others about the good news of Jesus Christ.

Advice to Reach Jews Today

I asked Steve how he would counsel a Christian who desired to witness to a Jew today. He gave us several insightful approaches.

"Too many Christians today are telling Jews they need to change or convert," Steve mused. "I don't want to tell a Jew that he has to stop being a Jew. I minister at a local nursing home that has a number of Jews, most of them not Christian. I ask them if I am any less Jewish since I am a Christian. They say, 'No, you're the biggest Jew we know!'"

Steve continued, "We don't need to be telling Jews about what will be taken away from them when they become Christian. We need to tell them how they will be fulfilled. I like using the word *fulfilled* rather than *completed* to describe Jews who have accepted Christ as their Messiah. *Completed* just doesn't work. All messianic Jews are works in progress, just like any other Christian."

> In any witnessing opportunity, the more Christians know about the beliefs of the person, the more effective they can be in sharing the gospel. In the case of Jews, it is not only good to know their beliefs, it is helpful to know their culture as well. A good resource is How to Respond to Judaism by Edwin Kolb and Erwin J. Kolb (Concordia Publishing House, 1995), a book that discusses both doctrinal and cultural issues.

I asked Steve if he had any other advice. "Realize," he said, "that most Jews today in America don't know Scripture. They only know their traditions. This gives you a great opportunity to show them things in the Old Testament. Take them to the book of Jeremiah [31:31–33] where the prophet said that God will give his people a new covenant, one that is not carved in tablets but etched in the heart. Then take them to the New Testament [2 Corinthians 3] and show them where Christ has given a new covenant.

"Also, take them to Isaiah 53. Show them the Suffering Servant and show them how Christ is the fulfillment of that.

"But the bottom line is to show them that God loves them, that he loves them unconditionally. When the Assembly of God pastor told me that God loves me, my whole life was shaken up. I guess that's what everyone needs to hear, both Jews and Gentiles alike."

The End of This Portion of the Journey

The evening was growing late. I was especially aware that Steve had to preach the next day. Maybe I was more concerned about myself. Frankly, I was having trouble keeping up with the energy and liveliness of my new friend. Perhaps I used the excuse of Steve's need for rest to cover my own decreasing stamina. I think Steve would have stayed up all night with no problem. Fortunately,

Nellie Jo and Deborah agreed with me. We all needed a good night's rest before the Saturday services of the next day.

Steve's story, like the Higleys' in Utah, had been an inspiration. I had heard once again how Christ had worked in a variety of ways through a number of people to introduce this Jewish man to his Savior.

Although Steve had studied the Scriptures with a zeal and intensity that would put most Christians to shame, the big moment of truth came when a young and inexperienced pastor told him that Jesus loved him. This theme of love permeates the interviews in this book. Mormons need to know that Jesus loves them. Jews need to know that Jesus loves them. And Christians must fearlessly, boldly, and enthusiastically tell a hurting world that Jesus loves them.

I paid the tab for the meal to two attractive Greek young ladies. I was told that they were the daughters of the owner. They giggled as I gave them my credit card. I sensed that their nervous laughter was an expression of relief that our table was finally cleared.

I looked at Steve. I saw his joy and his smile, and I felt his contagious enthusiasm. It was hard to imagine that I was looking at a man who had been suicidal with no hope in his life. I never cease to be amazed at what the love of Christ can do for someone.

Steve looked at me and said, "I am grateful for your time, Thom."

I responded, "We are all grateful for your time, Steve. It has been our honor to hear your story."

—◦◦◦—

My wife had to drive me home in a rental car because no driver's license meant no boarding of an airplane. But I was grateful for the time to reflect in the car. Most Christians would have considered Steve a lost cause before he became a Christian. Born in an Orthodox Jewish family, he was really a secular Jew before he trusted in his newfound Messiah.

Most people would have given up on him. Indeed, most Christians did. But a cute and determined blonde woman saw hope in her "project." A coworker prayed for him. And a pastor told Steve that Jesus loved him. A few cared. And a few made an eternal difference.

The weather was a bit chilly on the outside, but a bright ray of sunshine warmed me and put a smile on my face. But the smile was not just for the bright ray shining on me; it was also for the light that had come into Steve's life.

Life would resume its hectic normalcy for Nellie Jo and me as we returned to Louisville. But in just eleven days we would be sitting in a conference room listening to a former Hindu tell us how his life as a crippled young man would ultimately lead him to the Savior. Kansas City would be our next stop on this amazing and unexpected journey.

CHAPTER THREE

"I WENT FROM THE GUILT OF KARMA TO THE GRACE OF CHRIST"

A FORMER HINDU SHARES HIS JOURNEY

May 11
Kansas City, Missouri

I do not like early morning flights—especially those 6:00 a.m. flights for which I wake up at 3:30 a.m. and arrive at the airport at 5:00 a.m. At some point in my life, I changed from being a morning person to becoming a night person. Maybe the transition took place as I was trying to make publishers' deadlines for manuscripts in the late evening hours.

Not only did I have to deal with my own resistant body at 3:30 a.m., but I was responsible for waking up Nellie Jo. "Tell me again why we're trying to make this trip in just one day," she implored. I mumbled a response that did not even make sense to me.

By the time we arrived at Midwestern Baptist Theological Seminary in Kansas City later that morning, my wife and I were ready for an eight-hour nap. At least the weather gave the promise of a warm and sunny spring day.

We had an appointment with a professor and vice president at the seminary named N. S. R. K. Ravi. We later learned that the first four names were given to him at birth by a close relative. His last name, which is also his personal name, was given to him by his father.

In a Wheelchair but Standing Tall

A receptionist led us into a conference room. Dr. Ravi, we were told, would be out of his class in just a few minutes. We set up the recording equipment just as he entered the room. Ravi was in a wheelchair, but we soon forgot his disability. We were about to hear the story of a man who was truly a spiritual giant. He stood tall in our eyes.

After a few moments of small talk, we asked Ravi to begin his story early in his life. He obliged by taking us all the way back to his birth. And we soon learned why it was necessary to hear his complete biography.

From Powerful Caste to Outcast

When he was born in India in 1953, Ravi came into a family situation afforded only a relatively few persons in that nation. His family had wealth, and they also were in the second-highest caste, lower only than the priests. Ravi's life was one that seemed destined for comfort and opportunity. His family was also devout Hindu.

The village announcer proclaimed the birth of the baby boy. He invited everyone in the village to the *annaprasadam*, a festive distribution of food, on *namakarana*, the naming service on the twenty-first day after a baby is born. The family was rejoicing at the birth of a healthy son, especially since male children were seen as a treasure by the culture.

But at the age of three, Ravi was stricken with polio. He was among the last group of victims prior to the polio vaccine becoming available in India. His parents were devastated. They spent a fortune giving Ravi the best of medical treatment. At one point the young boy spent nine months in a total body cast. But his condition did not improve.

> *Hinduism is the third largest religion in the world. There are 800 million Hindus worldwide, 13 percent of the world's population. More than 80 percent of the people of India practice some form of Hinduism. In Nepal, Hinduism is the state religion, and 90 percent of the population is Hindu. There is no central headquarters or holy city. In fact, Hinduism really is not a single unified religion; rather, it is a tapestry of interwoven beliefs, most of which have their origin in the culture of India. Hinduism has no formal statements of belief or doctrine.*

Since the medical solutions were not fruitful, his parents turned to the village gods. His father had two expensive temples built for the gods, one of which still stands today. Nevertheless, there was no improvement in his condition. Though they kept him in their home, Ravi's parents began to see him as a burden. He had to have two people look after his needs, including one person who was responsible for carrying him wherever he needed to go.

> *The more common and fundamental principles of Hinduism are (1) a belief in reincarnation, (2) the worship of many and diverse gods that take on a variety of forms, and (3) belief in the essential spiritual unity of humankind.*

None of the gods had heard the prayers of Ravi's parents. His condition worsened, and he became completely disabled. After all of the work, sacrifices, and money spent on their son, his parents concluded that Ravi would not walk the rest of his life because he had bad karma in a previous life.

Nellie Jo and I looked at each other, and Ravi could see that we did not fully grasp what he was saying. "Karma is a Hindu fatalistic concept that necessitates reincarnation," he told us. "The conditions of each successive life are determined by one's bad or good deeds in past lives. It is kind of a universal law of cause and effect that determines fate or destiny. There is no forgiveness in karma. Each person must suffer for his own deeds of the past life. There is no innocent suffering in karma."

I waited a brief moment after he spoke. "Let me see if I got this right," I said. "You were being told as a young boy that you were crippled because of bad deeds you had committed in a previous life."

Ravi's sad nod told me that the pain of nearly a half century earlier had not been forgotten. "My father screamed at me one time: 'What kind of sins have you committed? You are nothing but a burden to us.'"

I had a lump in my throat trying to imagine a father saying such cruel words to his son.

"I was an outcast living with my own family," Ravi continued. "I grew bitter about my condition. None of the gods had helped me. My hatred toward the gods and my family grew stronger and stronger."

> Hinduism has countless gods in its belief system. But as the religion has developed, some of the earlier deities have disappeared and are no longer mentioned. Today there are three main gods among the many:
>
> 1. Brahma is the main god. He is also known as the Impersonal Absolute and the Ultimate Reality.
> 2. Vishnu is the god of all good causes. He has taken on human forms, the most popular of which is Krishna. Hare Krishna is the name of the movement that propagates this god.
> 3. Shiva is the god of creation and destruction, among other roles.

Ravi told us more of the difficulties of his childhood. "I saw how much my parents enjoyed my brothers and sisters, but they did not want to be around me. They would tell our housekeeper to carry me away from the rest of the family on special events. I was driven almost to the point of a nervous breakdown."

I could not imagine someone enduring such difficulties as a child. When Ravi was seventeen, he decided that he was at wits' end with his family. "At the age of seventeen, I stole some money and ran away from home. In the U.S. runaways are common, but it is almost unheard of in India," he told us.

Anyone who could see the events of Ravi's early life might question why he had to endure so much suffering. He could not have conceived at this point in his life that the one true God was working in these terrible times. The runaway child was soon to become a child of the King.

The ultimate goal of the Hindu is to attain *moksha*, the point when the soul unites with the Brahman, the Universal Soul or Ultimate Reality. This step will provide freedom from *samsara*, or the transmigration of the soul from one life to another (reincarnation). The process to break the cycle of reincarnation is to get more good karma than bad karma. This freedom takes place through good works, higher knowledge, and greater devotion. Simply stated, the better Hindu you are, the better your chances are of breaking the cycle.

From Bad Karma to Christ

"I had no idea what I was searching for when I ran away," Ravi recalled. "It was really a strange scene: a teenage boy in a wheelchair roaming the streets and the roads. One day I was just sitting on a bench at a train station, and a Christian dressed in a white robe sits down by me. I tried to lie and tell him that I was waiting for the next train, but he knew that wasn't the truth. The next train was not scheduled to arrive for another nine hours."

Ravi continued the story about the strange man at the train station. "He opened a Bible and just started sharing with me. Of course, I had no idea what he was talking about, but he kept reading and talking about verse after verse. I would see him close his eyes at times, but I had no idea what real prayer was."

"Was he sharing the gospel with you?" Nellie Jo asked.

"Probably," Ravi replied. "But I really didn't know what he was talking about at that point." He chuckled. "But he had a captive audience. I couldn't really go anywhere."

We all paused for a moment as a cacophony of voices could be heard outside the conference room. I surmised that classes were dismissing.

"This man just kept sharing with me," he continued. "He tried to persuade me that it was Adam's (I had no idea who that guy was) sin that tainted the entire human race, not the sins of my previous life. He told me that God really loves me, and how he paid for my sins. All of my life I had been told that the gods were angry with me since I did not please them enough."

The man was persistent with Ravi. "He repeated several times that God had a special purpose in my life, and that my physical disability would be used for God's glory," Ravi continued. "But I didn't even know what glory was."

Ravi said that the man stopped talking and prayed for him. Ravi told him that his parents had built temples for the gods, but they didn't hear the pleas of his mother and father. Why should this God hear his prayers? The man said without hesitation, "This is the true God who hears our prayers."

"Then the man prayed again," Ravi said with greater force. "This time when he finished praying, he opened the Bible to Psalm 27:10: 'When my father and mother forsake me, then the Lord will take me up.' It was amazing. That verse seemed to come out of the blue, but I could not get it out of my mind. For several months this verse was right in front of me. The words were ringing in my ears. Today I know the Holy Spirit engraved the Word of God on my heart to show that he truly loves me."

Although Ravi did not become a Christian that day, the strange man in white started a chain of events that would lead him to the

Savior. He told Ravi that he could go to a Christian boarding school about an hour away. They would take care of him and let him continue his education.

Fourteen months later in the Christian school, Ravi met Christ. "I finally understood sin, Romans 3:23. I finally understood that there is only one God, Isaiah 45:22. I saw that God had provided me a way of salvation through his Son Jesus Christ, John 3:16. And I read what I had to do to receive the Savior, Romans 10:13.

"After fourteen months of spiritual struggles and battles, I accepted Jesus Christ as my Lord and Savior. All of my sins were removed. What a freedom it was, and still is today," Ravi said with a smile that reflected his joy.

The greatest burden had been removed from Ravi's life. His sin had been taken away. He no longer had to worry about good and bad karma. And he saw that reincarnation was a total lie.

God Was Just Getting Started

The beginning of Ravi's new life as a Christian was not easy. The leaders at the Christian school insisted that the teenager write his parents and tell them what happened to him. He recalled their reaction sadly. "My parents told me that I had become an outcast by becoming a Christian. They told me that they would consider me as dead and that I was never to come home."

"What was your reaction?" I asked him.

"My anger started to get the best of me. But the leaders at the school told me that I had to forgive them and keep writing to them. After a few letters, the love and forgiveness began to flow naturally. I started loving them. For seven years I kept writing them, but they still disowned me. I was never invited to a family function."

Ravi did see some signs of hope. "My mother would find ways to get money to me and to make sure I was okay," he said with a smile.

Nellie Jo returned the smile. "Mamas are like that," she said.

"But my mother had to do that without my father knowing," Ravi told us. "He was still so angry with me and felt shame about me for what I did."

Ravi wondered what God had planned for him. He was getting close to graduating from college, and he had job offers waiting. One of the more attractive offers with a large corporation was tempting, but he could get no peace about accepting the job. His restlessness and uncertainty continued while he was attending convocation (similar to a revival) at the school.

"I kept sensing God was calling me to preach, but I would tell him that I couldn't preach because I was a cripple and couldn't stand," Ravi recalled. "Then one night during convocation, I read the passage of Scripture from Micah 4:6–7: 'In that day,' declares the LORD, 'I will gather the lame; I will assemble the exiles and those I have brought to grief. I will make the lame a remnant, those driven away a strong nation. The LORD will rule over them in Mount Zion from that day and forever.'

"That did it for me," said Ravi. "I wasn't sure what I would do next, but I determined that I would train for the ministry." Through a series of God-provided miracles, Ravi moved to the United States and attended seminary. He has held many high-profile ministry positions in America, including his present role as vice president and professor at Midwestern Baptist Theological Seminary in Kansas City.

When More Hindus Become Christians

Ravi told us how he met his wife in India and how the two of them and their child came to America. The stories were fascinating, but I was eager to hear more about his immediate family, all of whom were Hindu. "What happened to your parents spiritually?" I asked.

The big grin on Ravi's face gave the answer, but he also told us the full story of how that happened. "While I was still living in India," he told us, "I began to see my mother from time to time. She would see something different in me and tell my father about me."

"After we moved to the United States," he said, "I began praying every day for my parents to become Christians. After seventeen years, I had a great burden to visit my parents in India. So I called my parents. My father answered, and I said, 'Daddy, I want to come see you.' He tried to find excuses for me not to come, but he finally said okay.

"After we arrived in India, I met alone with my parents," he continued. "It didn't take me long to ask my father a straightforward question: 'Daddy, do you have peace in your heart?' My father responded with a huff, 'What do you mean do I have peace in my heart? I go to the temple every day.' I told my father that I had been praying for him for seventeen years, and I wanted him to know how to have peace."

> Polytheism, the belief in many gods, is a central belief in Hinduism. Different gods perform different functions. None of the gods are personal. Essentially, Hindus decide on the god or gods they want, and they can choose what they want to believe.

Ravi continued with his story, "My mother started crying. She said, 'I can see the God you worship is different from our gods. He has changed your life. He has helped you so much in life. Our gods do not help us.'"

Then Ravi's father started sobbing as well. "For the first time in many years," Ravi said softly, "I hugged my parents. I said, 'Can we ask my God to come into your lives?' They both kept crying, even as they accepted Christ. What a glorious day May 30, 1987, was. On that afternoon my parents became children of my God and my Savior."

The evidence of Ravi's parents' salvation became immediately apparent. His father stopped going to the temples and destroyed his idols. He no longer supported the temples, even those he built. And his life was one decidedly different and better than when he was a Hindu.

"Daddy died in 2001," Ravi shared with us. "I got to visit him and spent three of the closest days of my life with him just three months before he died. Even though he was facing death, he had a joy that he had never known in his years as a Hindu.

"If you want to see the fruits of Hinduism, go to a Hindu funeral. When there is death, everyone cries as if there is no hope. But my daddy told me that he didn't want anyone crying at his funeral. He just wanted a celebration. And you have never seen such a celebration as that funeral. We fed the entire village, and there was celebration and dancing for hours. The Hindus in the village saw what a Christian funeral was like; they saw the joy," Ravi recalled with a smile.

The Hindus Next Door

The next series of questions were both for this book and for me personally. A few years ago, a young Hindu couple moved next door to our family. Since they have become my neighbors, they have been blessed with the birth of a daughter.

Both the young man and the young woman have been exceedingly nice to us. In fact, we could not ask for more pleasant neighbors. Nellie Jo and I enjoy speaking to them on those rare occasions when we are at home.

But I have a confession. I have done little to engage them in conversations of spiritual issues. Here I am writing a book on the unexpected journeys of people from other belief systems, and I have done little to intentionally reach the Hindus next door. Now, I could offer you some excuses about my travel schedules. Or I could tell you how incredibly busy we are when we are at home. But those are excuses. Weak excuses. Can I really say that anything is more important than the eternal destiny of someone?

Perhaps one reality that many American Christians recognize only superficially is the increasing religious plurality in the United States. Hindus number 1.8 million in America, and the Muslims outnumber them. There are more Jews in America than in Israel.

Six million Mormons live in the United States, and nearly 1 million Jehovah's Witnesses.

I could continue to list other beliefs and religious systems in the United States, but just those numbers are clear evidence that it is a nation of many religions. Thus, when I write about Hindus in America, I am not writing about some abstract concept that will never be a part of my life. For me the Hindus are next door; our homes are separated by some sixty feet of grass.

As I began to ask Ravi questions about reaching Hindus in America, I listened closely. I wanted material for this book, and I wanted to become effective in reaching my own neighbors.

> Hinduism in America is growing. Around 1.8 million Hindus live in the United States. They are concentrated in major metropolitan areas such as New York City, Los Angeles, and San Francisco.

Reaching Hindus in America: The Foundation of Love

"How do you begin to share the gospel with a Hindu in America?" I asked Ravi.

"Though you want to share verbally the gospel as soon as possible," he responded, "you have to build a foundation first. All Hindus, including those in America, watch closely how people live their lives. The typical Hindu has a very disciplined life; they work very hard. And they observe your life as well."

Nellie Jo interjected, "What are they looking for?"

Ravi paused for a moment and then resumed. "Above all, you just need to show Christ's love. If you do that, you will soon win the audience of American Hindus."

I could tell Nellie Jo and I were thinking the same thing, so I verbalized the question: "But what do we do if we mess up? No Christian is perfect. Have we lost any chance to influence a Hindu?"

"No, not all," Ravi responded. "Just apologize. Tell them you messed up when you do something wrong. They will be quick to embrace you. Apologies are a big thing in Hindu culture. Most Hindus are loving and caring, and they will be impressed by your humility."

Ravi's eyes widened as he began to share his own evangelistic work among his Hindu relatives and friends in America. "I have had the opportunity to share the gospel with many Hindus in the U.S.," he said with enthusiasm. "Some of my own relatives here ask me how I live a life of joy and happiness. They see my disability, but they see no anger or resentment. They see a different kind of joy-filled life. Sharing the gospel with them is easy—they ask me all the questions."

"But how about us who have no Hindu relatives or friends?" I asked Ravi. "You obviously have greater opportunities because you are a former Hindu."

Ravi would not let me shirk my responsibility for reaching Hindus. "It's really simple," he retorted. "Ask a Hindu to dinner or into your home. Most Hindus love fellowship once you know them and they know you. They will usually respond enthusiastically and invite you into their homes as well. Hospitality is a big thing in the Hindu culture. There is really no reason for a Christian not to establish a relationship with a Hindu."

Having felt rightfully humbled, I was quiet. Nellie Jo picked up the conversation. "Once we have a Hindu in our home, or if we go into their home, what do we say?"

Ravi responded, "First, realize that most of the Hindus will consider it a great honor to have fellowship with you. They will go out of their way to please you; they will make sacrifices to make you comfortable. You will not be in an antagonistic setting; to the contrary, you will find them very receptive to your conversations."

Ravi could tell that Nellie Jo and I were already imagining having our neighbors in our home. We both seemed to be wondering how the conversation would develop. Ravi anticipated our next questions.

Conversing with a Hindu

"Begin the conversation by asking them questions," he told us. "Just simply ask them about their background. Ask them to explain the caste system in India. Most Hindus will gladly take the conversation from there. They are honored that you are interested in them."

Ravi continued, "At some point in the conversation, ask them about their own practices of worship. They may even show you a small place in their home, like a closet, where they worship their gods.

"At some point in the conversation about worship, you could ask them how they feel when they pray, what they expect from their gods. You see, a Hindu is begging the gods to provide for them. This gives you a great opportunity to share about how Christians pray. You are able to tell them how Christ always hears the prayers of Christians and always wants his best for them. Then you can gently share about the love of Christ."

> Some of the influences of Hinduism in the West are already a part of many persons' vocabulary and lives. For example, the word **mantra** is commonly used in America to indicate the repetition of a word or a phrase. This term has its origins in Hinduism with those who practice transcendental meditation. It means to chant or repeat words in order to invoke the presence of a particular god. The word **karma** also is becoming more common in the American vocabulary. Many people use the word to indicate bad or good fortune, but as noted earlier, the word is closely associated with the Hindu concept of reincarnation.

Ravi repeated a caution to us several times: "You must never condemn them or act judgmental toward them. Hindus respond best to open conversations and friendliness. They are willing to hear you out on almost anything as long as you listen to them and are interested in them."

"Are there any other particular points of discussion on which you would offer advice?" I asked.

"Yes," Ravi responded. "Most Hindus have a great difficulty understanding the concept of sin and the origin of the first karma. I have had great success in just opening the Bible and showing them what it says about sin. I then ask them if they feel clean when they go to the temple or when they perform their rituals. Most of them will admit that they don't. That is a great opportunity to explain what Christ did for the sins of the world."

Even though the recorder was running, I was taking notes furiously. I was already thinking about how I could apply some of these concepts with my next-door neighbors. While I was writing, Ravi offered another suggestion.

"You can also ask them what their ultimate goal in life is," he added. "Most American Hindus are cultural Hindus. They are becoming more secular and materialistic. You will be amazed how many will respond positively if you show them in Scripture how we can be with the one true God forever, that we do not have to go through an endless cycle of lives where we become one with false gods."

When Hindus Become Christians

I was curious about Ravi's mother. He had already shared with us about the conversion of both of his parents and about his father's death. So I asked him how his mother was doing.

"She had heart failure a few years ago," he said with apparent love for his mother. "But she told all of her relatives that God was going to let her live longer to share the love of Christ with others. She is living on borrowed time now, but she continues to be a great witness for the gospel."

The mention of his mother and her conversion triggered one related thought. "When a Hindu tells you that he or she has accepted Christ," Ravi forewarned, "that person may not be a Christian. A Hindu can just count Christ as one of many gods. Follow-up is critical. You have to find out if that person has truly accepted Christ as the one true God."

From False Gods to One True God

Once again the time for an interview had passed quickly. I looked at the former Hindu in the wheelchair. I did not see a person who thought life had given him a bad deal. I did not see a man who questioned the love of God. I did not see an individual who, because of his disability, viewed life as hopeless and meaningless. On the contrary, I saw a man who radiated the love of Christ, who was amazed that the love of Christ had found him as a bitter runaway teenage Hindu in India. I saw inescapable joy.

———

I left that interview with a new determination, in God's power, to reach my own Hindu neighbors. We interviewed a changed man, and in many respects, I left a changed man.

The late spring afternoon warmth welcomed us as Nellie Jo and I exited the building. Another unexpected journey had taught us much and, just as important, had inspired us greatly.

In just over two weeks we would be traveling to a western Pennsylvania town outside Pittsburgh. This time we would not be interviewing a person who had become a Christian from another false god. We would interview a woman who became a Christian from a belief that no god existed. She was an atheist. As a matter of fact, she was an atheist who despised Christians. But, in my enthusiasm, I am getting ahead of myself. That story ensues in the next chapter.

CHAPTER FOUR

"THE WORST IDIOTS WERE CHRISTIANS"

FROM ATHEISM TO CHRISTIANITY

May 27
Greensburg, Pennsylvania

Driving to Pennsylvania was my idea, and it was not a bright idea at all. I looked at flight times and driving distances to Greensburg, Pennsylvania, and I rationalized that driving was the easiest and most economical route to go. I was wrong.

I must confess that if driving to Pennsylvania had been Nellie Jo's idea, I would have complained for hours about her poor decision making. Fortunately, my wife did not ever say, "I told you so," but I did feel pretty stupid about my decision.

The MapQuest program on my computer told me that the drive from Louisville would be a mere 407.56 miles. I had driven further. No problems this time, but I hadn't accounted for construction on every other road and a poorly marked toll road.

The story of the toll road could fill this chapter, which would be counter to the purpose of the project, so let me see if I can quickly summarize the story. I got my ticket at the toll booth, and I was told that I would pay after I exited the toll road. Somehow,

I ended up at the original toll booth. I had gone in a circle for forty miles. You should have seen the look on the booth operator's face when the card reader indicated I had been zero miles!

The various delays put us in our motel room at 1:30 a.m. But the frustration I had experienced that evening would soon be forgotten. Nellie Jo and I were about to hear of an astonishing and unexpected journey from atheism to Christianity.

Meet Mrs. Jones

Mrs. A. S. A. Jones worked in a social charitable organization in Greensburg. While Nellie Jo and I did not get to spend much time in Greensburg, we both were impressed with the neatness of the town about one hour east of Pittsburgh.

I was not certain how we would be received by Mrs. Jones. Of all the interviews we conducted, she was the most reticent to talk with us. We would soon learn that she was concerned about me and my reputation as a writer. "Atheists can be a suspicious and critical lot. They like to believe that anyone claiming to be an atheist wasn't really an atheist in the first place. I don't want them attacking your integrity should they attempt to discredit me," she would tell us shortly.

Nellie Jo and I found her office, and she welcomed us with a smile that seemed to have a mischievous edge to it. We took an immediate liking to this woman. She encouraged us to address her by her nickname in the office, "Mrs. J.," and we complied happily. After our brief introductions, I asked her to tell her story, the story of her unexpected journey from atheism to Christianity.

"I was raised a Roman Catholic in a home where Jesus Christ and God were never mentioned," Mrs. J. began. Both Nellie Jo and I were not surprised to hear her talk about her home life. Throughout her office were photographs of her family.

She continued, "Prayer was never a part of my home life either. My mother attended church regularly, but my father only attended on Easter and Christmas. There was no consistency in the religion they said they believed and the way their faith demonstrated itself. Although I was encouraged to attend catechism and church every weekend, the concept of God was never made completely real to me.

> Atheism is a term originally used in Greece to designate the belief of those who did not believe in the official gods of the state, whether or not they believed in any other type of god. The term "atheist" comes from the Greek word theos, which means "god." Add the prefix a, which means "without" or "not," and you have the word atheos. Atheist thus literally means "without God."

"By the time I was thirteen, I had concluded that God was merely a vicious adult version of the Easter bunny. I abandoned the lie, informed my upset parents that I would no longer be attending church, and began seeking truth," she said softly.

Now, if you had been in the office with Mrs. J., you would have noticed something as quickly as Nellie Jo and I did. This woman is very smart. She majored in biology in college, and she is extremely well read. I could imagine this young teenager declaring to her parents her philosophical intent to pursue other sources of truth.

Mrs. J. confirmed our suspicions about her intellect. "At the age of sixteen," she offered matter-of-factly, "my IQ and my grades made me eligible for my high school's early release program, and I began my studies in biology and chemistry at the University of Pittsburgh."

Morality Crumbles without a Foundation

"For most of my youth, I accepted the moral values of my parents," she continued. "But once I abandoned the myth of God, I had no basis upon which to build my morality. Without the concept of a higher authority, morality is admittedly relative. I remember staring at a swarming mass of termites one day, thinking that from a comparative distance, there was little difference between them and us. I smashed a few dozen with my shoe and ground them into the dirt. What did it matter if they all died? People die every day. The end result would always be death for both the individuals and, eventually, the species. You see, even the ethics of murder can be challenged and reduced to subjective opinion. Why should mankind consider life sacred, knowing that its preservation is an exercise in futility?"

The downward spiral of her views on morality continued. "Humanity had become nothing more to me than an organized network of molecules and enzymes," she said. "I viewed people as mere organisms going through their daily routines of metabolizing nutrients and expelling wastes, ovulating their eggs and ejaculating their semen."

Christians and Other Idiots

The rationalism that Mrs. J embraced rejected all beliefs of an objective truth and God. Indeed, she began turning against Christians. "The worst idiots were the Christians," she told us. "I hated them because, in their ignorance of naturalism, they failed to see that there was no reason for the rest of the world to believe in their God. Their pretentiousness sickened me, despite my being equally pretentious toward them. I thought I was justified in my pretentiousness! At least I could give logical reasons for not believing in the supernatural."

The hatred that Mrs. J. had toward Christians was often demonstrated in overt acts against them. "I worked in an office with a born-again Christian," she began.

Nellie Jo interjected, "Did you consider him a fanatic?"

Her response was quick, "Sure, a fanatic is anyone who is more religious than you are," she chuckled.

Mrs. J.'s acts of cruelty toward her coworker were numerous. "I would bring *The Satanic Bible* to work just to tick him off," she recalled. "One time he brought a plastic model of a fetus to work. I wore it on top of my head for a while."

> *Most definitions of atheism have not changed over the years. It is simply the denial or disbelief in the existence of God or a supreme intelligent being.*

Her antagonism against Christians went unabated for years. "I loved debating Christians," she recalled. "I would trip them up on logical inconsistencies. I tried to make fools of them. Most Christians were easy targets. They had less familiarity with the Bible than I did."

Mrs. J. continued, "My anti-Christian arguments became my ultimate diversion to a hopeless life. To justify my desire to destroy Christianity, I had to find reasons to discredit it. I railed against its hypocrisy and the behavior of its followers."

An Unexpected Journey to the Bible

How could someone who had intellectually convinced herself that God did not exist come to believe that there is a God and that he revealed himself through his Son, Jesus Christ? The cliché was true for Mrs. J., for God was truly working in mysterious ways in her life.

> *The estimated number of atheists in America is around one million. Among atheists there are two broad groups. One category is the "weak-position" atheists who do not believe in God because they have never seen credible evidence that God exists. "Strong-position" atheists are adamant that there is no God. They are firmly opposed to theists in general and to Christians in particular.*

"One day I had an argument with a Christian," she began. "He told me that I was missing the entire point of Christianity by arguing every point. I thought about what he said, and it really irked me. But I couldn't get his words out of my mind. I began to ask myself, *What if he is right? Maybe I am reading the Bible the wrong way.*

"I made a resolution on New Year's Day 1998 to read the entire Bible again. I had read it through many times before, but as one would read a technical manual or a science book. It occurred to me that I was perhaps missing points that were being delivered through nuance and context—the type of literary devices that are used in higher forms of literature. I started in Genesis and began to read. This book began to read me as I was reading it."

Mrs. J. would struggle with some of the stories of Scripture. "But every time I found fault with this God, I ended up finding fault with myself. When I would condemn this God for commanding Moses to kill, I began to ask how I even had any standards of morality by which to judge the action. Was I not contradicting my own position that there are no absolutes?"

Mrs. J.'s demeanor had changed. The conversation had begun somewhat subdued and soft-spoken. She was now becoming more animated with each sentence. "I then got to the question Christ asked: 'Who do you say that I am?' After six months of reading Scripture, that one question summed it all up for me. I finally realized that what I had to say about Christ said more about me than him. I felt this small." She raised her thumb and index finger to indicate the smallness she felt.

It is difficult for me to communicate well what was taking place in that office during the interview. If ever someone would have been declared hopeless and godless, it was Mrs. A. S. A. Jones. Once again Nellie Jo and I knew that we were hearing the testimony of an amazing miracle.

Allow me to fast-forward a few days before I return to this incredible journey. Three days after we returned to Louisville, I read Mrs. J.'s written testimony. This is how she describes her encounter with Christ even more fully:

"At this moment," she wrote, "I saw it. I saw what the truth of the Bible was! And I was humbled. The truth of the Bible was and is Jesus Christ!"

The text continued, "The moment I was made aware of my despicable nature, I realized that Jesus had died for me. I never had recognized sin and therefore thought that Christ had died for nothing. But this man was able to see through the horrible nature present in all humanity, yet he sacrificed himself to save us. In a very real sense, my sinful nature had caused the death of an innocent man. I never believed in hell prior to this, but one of my first thoughts, after seeing how hellish a person I was, was that I deserved to be in it."

In the dimly lit room, she expounded, "I had seen myself as perfect; I was the standard by which others should be judged! I thought that my intelligence would make me a bastion of moral clarity. But all those thoughts and delusions immediately vanished when I reviewed my life in the context of there being a Christian God. I fell so short of that standard. By July 1998 I began to see and accept the God of the Bible."

There was no doubt in her office that morning. Mrs. J. was a believer in Jesus Christ. "I really fell in love with him. I really fell in love with Jesus," she said more softly.

From an Atheist to an Apologist

"My temptation was to tell as many people as I could about Jesus. I wanted to get on the Internet and warn other atheists that they were going to hell," she laughed. "But I soon regained my composure and realized that if I did that, they would look at me just as I had looked at other Christians. They would think I was an idiot now."

Nellie Jo inquired, "What did you do next?"

Mrs. J. responded, "Well, I told my parents what had happened. My mother wanted to know why I had to be a born-again Christian, as if that was the worst possible type of Christian anyone could choose to be," she said with a hint of sarcasm.

She continued, "I also began studying the Bible more deeply, but this time from my new perspective as a Christian. I had read other books of other religions. They were typically redundant statements of man's moral opinions. I found them to be either incomplete because they provided no reason for me to accept the opinions or difficult to accept as true because of the known deceptive nature of their prophet. But I believe that the Bible describes a very real God because of the way in which it was revealed. It's as if its prophets were given separate pieces of a jigsaw puzzle and, with no understanding of how they would fit together, accurately described them. The pieces of the puzzle were delivered over a span of fifteen hundred years and through over forty different authors, yet they come together in a way that makes sense. When they are viewed in the light of their entirety, they document man's struggle with his own nature, the nature of the God that he worships, and the final solution to his selfish condition. That's why the Bible is said to be authored by God, because it is as if the text was designed and directed by one source, a source that had to know the end of the book from its beginning."

Nellie Jo asked if Mrs. J. did any reading of books on Christian apologetics at this point.

"No," she said with a grin, "I wanted to create my own apologetics."

She could tell that neither Nellie Jo nor I understood what she meant, so she explained. "I had been in conversations with Christians for years," she noted, "especially with the availability of the Internet. I had done everything I could to destroy them and their arguments. Now I had this great opportunity to go back to the Internet and defend Christianity. The atheistic community is tough. I really wanted to see if my intellect could embrace my faith. So I began arguing with them on message boards and in forums. My arguments held and my faith was strengthened."

"Did you start going to church?" I asked. I could tell that this question was not an unemotional issue for her.

"No, I didn't go to church for a few years. I knew a lot about what church was like and I didn't know if my infant faith could survive it," she declared.

> Because naturalism excludes God, it is the worldview that most atheists hold. Naturalism maintains that reality is limited to material elements and nature. Matters such as morality are relative because there are no absolute truths or moral standards. Theists, persons who believe in the existence of any type of god, are dismissed by atheists because theists do not accept the certain reality that God does not exist.

"Ouch," I thought to myself.

Mrs. J. did eventually seek a church home. She found a non-denominational church close to where she lives. "The first Sunday I walked into that church, I thought, 'I'm home.' I have been there ever since. And the born-again guy that I made miserable is a member there too."

In her written testimony, Mrs. J. tells about the life changes that began to take place. "The most outstanding change that took place in me was that I was freed from my cold indifference in matters of heart," she wrote. "My atheistic philosophy had allowed me to lose my compassion for others. I no longer had the ability to love anyone, even myself."

She continued, "Jesus Christ restored my heart and my conscience. Christians speak of this as a veil being lifted, but for me it was more like the iron curtain was being torn down. For the first time in my life, I was seeing the world as it really was."

The story of Mrs. A. S. A. Jones's conversion is the story of the power of Scripture to pierce the heart of even someone who claims there is no God. And her story is one of a relentless God who pursued her even when she did not believe he existed. It is truly an incredible and unexpected journey.

But we had come to hear the story of her journey and to get counsel on how to reach atheists today. While their numbers are not huge relative to the population of America, their worldview is increasingly influential.

Christians Reaching Out to Atheists

Atheism denies the existence of any supernatural being above humanity. There is no transcendent order or meaning in the universe to atheists. For these people, any notion of a god is wishful and fictional thinking. From a human perspective, sharing the love and gospel of Christ is an exceedingly difficult task. Mrs. J.'s testimony had made that reality abundantly clear.

But part of her testimony did include a comment from a Christian that drove her to study the Bible with a different mental framework. It was in that study that she felt compelled to answer Christ's question, "Who do you say that I am?"

So I asked her straightforwardly, "How should a Christian witness to an atheist?"

She responded quickly, "Too many Christians want to engage atheists with an arsenal of apologetics. It's like feeding junk food to people who need real nourishment."

Recalling her own atheistic beliefs, she continued speaking. "Look, I used to destroy apologetic arguments when I debated Christians. Most atheists have read all the same apologetics literature as the Christian, if not a whole lot more. They are prepared for about anything you can throw at them."

"Are you saying that none of these arguments are valid?" I asked.

"It isn't a matter of validating or invalidating arguments," she responded. "It is about being able to see those same arguments from a different perspective. A person can offer a disagreement, but a disagreement doesn't constitute invalidation. Because neither can objectively prove their points, both Christians and atheists walk away from debates confident that they have won."

I was curious about her comments. "Are you saying that apologetics have no value in witnessing to atheists?" I asked.

"They can have value," she countered. "But my experience tells me that a change of heart must precede any intellectual receptivity to Christian arguments. No amount of debates could have convinced me that God or Christ is real. What I discovered was an intellectual riddle that couldn't be solved by the logical mind. It had to be solved by the intuitive heart.

"When Christians start regurgitating intelligent design arguments, or attempt to disprove evolution, or begin citing every extant manuscript to prove the historicity of Jesus, I have to ask, did they learn of these things before they acquired faith, and did these things thus cause them to have faith? Or, more likely, did they already have faith, and then later learn of these things and then apply them to arguments to justify their faith?" She paused thoughtfully. "The best arguments for the existence of God come from those who know exactly what they believe."

The Best Argument for Belief

"What is your best argument for belief?" I asked.

"Atheists think that faith is belief without reason," she responded. "But my faith is based upon the trustworthy character of Christ. Quite frankly, the words of Christ are unlike any other words I have read."

She continued, "Also, because I find the Bible to be verifiably true in its major themes, I trust it to be true when it comes to the existence of God, which I cannot verify. The authors seem to be consumed by their efforts to define morality and truth. I cannot imagine that they would knowingly tell lies that would bring harm to them and to those believing them. My faith is not based on lofty academic arguments. It is based on the personal experience of connecting with the living mind of Christ."

Lifestyle Witness versus a Verbal Witness

A major theme of our interviews was how Christians must model the love of Christ in order to have an audience with those who are not Christians. I asked if that issue applied to her.

"I didn't see a lot of Christian love when I was an atheist. I became a Christian despite Christians," she reflected.

For me that statement was another "ouch moment," an indictment against unloving and uncaring Christians.

Catching my expression, Mrs. J. added quickly, "Oh, not what you think! I could find fault with anyone, even the people whom I now see as loving and Christlike. The problem was with me, not Christians. But even if I could have recognized Christ's love in Christians, it would not have brought me one step closer to the conclusion that God actually existed."

A. S. A. Jones's journey from atheism was proving itself to be an exception to the norm. "Are you saying that the love of Christians played no part in your conversion?" I asked.

"Exactly," Mrs. J. replied. "It would be a logical fallacy to believe that God existed just because Christians were loving and well-behaved. A Hindu may be kind and loving, but that wouldn't speak for the validity of Krishna's existence."

Time was slipping away too quickly. The place where Mrs. J. worked was abuzz with activity and conversations. I did not want to be presumptuous of her time, but I still needed clarification. "Could Christians have said or done anything differently to prompt your journey toward faith?" I asked.

Mrs. Jones hesitated. "I didn't need the love of Christ as much as I needed his offensive judgment. What I really needed was a Christian who had the guts to tell me that I wasn't the marvelous and upstanding person I considered myself to be. I needed someone to cut me down to size, but my ego had grown so large that the only person big enough to do that was Christ himself."

Things You Just Have to Know

Mrs. J. told us that Christians are woefully lacking in knowledge of Scripture. She read the Bible cover to cover many times while she was an atheist. But she debated with Christians whose scriptural knowledge was woefully lacking. Although the point may seem self-evident, Christians must know the Bible if they are to defend the faith with clarity and conviction.

Christians must also get beyond the stereotypes of people of other beliefs. "I run into a lot of Christians who think that all atheists are immoral. That is not necessarily true," Mrs. J. told us. "I was an atheist who, for many years, held to traditional biblical moral beliefs just because they were the beliefs of my parents." Though her moral standards would later crumble without a certain foundation, her point was well made. Not all atheists are alike.

> Atheists see humans as part of random evolutionary development. Humans were not created; they just happened. The only superiority humans have over other species is that we are above the evolutionary chain. We can solve the problems of the world with our superior intelligence.

Mrs. J. also shared with us that there are two major categories of atheists. One group is apathetic toward religions. They do not believe in the existence of God, but neither do they have an agenda to further their beliefs in a world without God.

The other group of atheists is a part of a well-connected atheistic community. "Do they have an agenda?" Nellie Jo asked.

"Oh, yes," Mrs. J. responded emphatically. "They have a very clear agenda. They want to destroy Christianity."

Nellie Jo and I stared in amazement at her statement. I can only imagine what she saw in our faces.

"They view Christians and the church as all that is wrong with society today," she told us. "A number of the atheists are also a part of the active homosexual community or are deeply involved in pro-choice politics. Many are filled with hatred for what they see as the condemning and restricting values of the Christian community. I know how they feel. As an atheist with a political ax to grind, I looked at all the churches on nearly every street corner and said, 'My God, they are everywhere.' Now I look at those same churches and wonder if there are any Christians of conviction in them."

She continued, "The bottom line is that there are a large number of atheists who hate Christians. They feel that if they can destroy Christianity, they will no longer have to live in a society where their lives are regulated by laws that reflect Christian values."

As I listened to her words, I realized that I was not hearing the speculative musings of someone who was talking about some other group. She had been there. She had done that. She had hated Christians. She had denied the existence of God with every fiber of her being.

I hope that as you read this book and hear these stories, you will be aware of the marvelous power of Christ to change lives. Listen to more of Mrs. J.'s written testimony.

"For me," she said, "biblical truth wasn't verified through the historical accuracy, inerrancy, or reliability of the Gospels, because my initial assumptions didn't include these things. I saw divine inspiration in the actual content of the words attributed to Jesus Christ. The fact that I, or anyone, was capable of understanding spiritual matters became evidence for my soul."

She continued, "Learning the things of the Spirit dramatically changed my attitude and outlook on life. It wasn't that the information available to me had changed, but that my perception had changed and, as a result, I was changed. I was dead, but Christ woke me up! He saved me from my selfish self, and I have given myself to him because I am thankful for that which he has given me and hopeful for that which he has promised."

A Very, Very Real God

The time to leave had come. Nellie Jo and I again stood amazed at the awesome power of God to transform even the most resistant of persons. Mrs. A. S. A. Jones was not just someone who once had not trusted Christ as her Savior; just a few years earlier she had been an atheist who despised Christians and their values.

As I turned off the recorder and began gathering my notes, I looked across the desk at this woman who had fallen in love with

Christ. I wondered how many people in my past I had considered hopeless. I wondered how many times I had given up on people whom God was not about to abandon.

Mrs. J.'s testimony of that relentless God still echoes in my mind today. "I became aware of my soul and how dirty it was when the light of Christ fell upon it," she said. "My accusing finger turned around and pointed right at me. Christianity wasn't what was wrong with the world. A lack of education wasn't what was wrong with the world. I was what was wrong with the world."

The God of all power began a work in Mrs. J. that continues to this day. "I prayed for forgiveness to a God whose existence I had thought was intellectually indefensible," she noted. "But he was very, very real. Within days almost every viewpoint I had once so loudly announced changed. I could no longer justify my advocacy of abortion, homosexuality, or premarital sex because I recognized these options for what they were, that being selfishness."

What began as conversation with others to hear about their journeys had now become a journey for Nellie Jo and me. We could not listen to these people without seeing their changed lives. And we could not listen to them without our own lives being changed.

After we bid farewell to Mrs. J., we walked to the parking lot. I was grateful that the day was bright and sunny. Perhaps this time I would not spend nearly an hour going in a circle on the toll road.

"You know," Nellie Jo commented. "My own faith is growing as I hear these testimonies. I wouldn't trade these days for anything."

My wife was right. But the journey was still in its early stages. Unfortunately, the journey was delayed for more than two months. I did not expect to have surgery during this venture, but life is not always as smooth as we would like it.

That is certainly a lesson we learned from a former Jehovah's Witness in West Virginia. Before he became a Christian, he and his wife were confronted with an agonizing choice. Would they be faithful to their religion and not allow their young daughter to have a blood transfusion, resulting in her likely death? Or would they deny their religion to save their daughter? That remarkable story is next.

CHAPTER FIVE

"THEY LET MY DAUGHTER DIE"

A TURBULENT JOURNEY FROM JEHOVAH'S WITNESSES TO CHRIST

August 9
Beckley, West Virginia

Among the people Nellie Jo and I interviewed, we heard about some powerful and unexpected journeys. For me, the progress on the project had become an interrupted journey. Fully recovered from surgery and eager to get to work, I prepared for a trip to Beckley, West Virginia. Since West Virginia is a neighboring state to Kentucky, I once again chose to drive rather than fly. This trip would not be as delay-filled as our previous journey, but it did prove to be interesting.

Russ Kreuter, my graduate assistant, joined Nellie Jo and me on the drive to West Virginia. We saw three accidents take place right in front of our vehicle on three separate occasions. And we saw a distracted truck driver run over some twenty construction pylons. Fortunately, no one was hurt in any of the incidents, and we made our appointment at the designated time.

A Town Named Beckley, a Man Named Paul

Named for John Beckley, the first clerk of Congress during the administrations of Presidents Washington, Adams, and Jefferson, the town of Beckley, West Virginia, is fast becoming an area known for its tourist attractions. Just minutes from the town of nearly 20,000 is whitewater rafting on the oldest river in North America, the New River. For winter enthusiasts, some of the best snow skiing areas in this region of the United States are just fifteen miles away.

But on this late summer day, the three of us were not in Beckley to enjoy its rivers or mountains. We had come to hear an extraordinary story about an extraordinary man named Paul.

He has that contagious enthusiasm that makes you feel like you know him well after just a few minutes. And his story is so captivating that hours seem like minutes. Paul Blizard is now a Baptist pastor. But just years ago, he was viewed by many within the organization as a promising leader for Jehovah's Witnesses. His story is one we will not forget.

> Jehovah's Witnesses started in 1872 when Charles T. Russell began predicting that Christ was going to return to earth and establish a millennial kingdom in 1914.

Paul welcomed us eagerly and took us into his office. His shelves were filled with a plethora of Jehovah's Witnesses' books and unusual souvenirs. Among those unusual items were autographs of several U.S. presidents and a photograph of Paul meeting with the late Yasir Arafat. My wife noticed something else on the shelves.

"I see a lot of UK [University of Kentucky] items," Nellie Jo commented. "Are you a Big Blue fan?" Paul responded with enthusiasm, "Absolutely! But my son graduated from the University of Louisville. He's the black sheep of the family."

But we were not there to admire office items. We were all eager to begin the interview.

"Paul," I said as I turned on the recorder, "we are here to hear your story. Begin wherever you desire. We will interrupt only when we want you to expand on something or provide clarification." We sat back and began to hear the amazing story of an unexpected journey to faith in Christ.

> There are 6 million Jehovah's Witnesses worldwide in 230 countries; about 1 million of them reside in the United States.

A Third-Generation Jehovah's Witness

"Look at all the Jehovah's Witnesses' books on my shelves," Paul said, waving his arm at the volumes. "When I became a Christian, I burned everything I had on the organization. It has taken me years to rebuild my library, but now I have everything I lost plus more. I have a deep history in the organization."

Paul continued, "My grandfather became a Jehovah's Witness under the teaching of Charles Taze Russell, the founder of the group. So my mother was raised as a Witness, and I was born into a solid Jehovah's Witnesses family. My family is linked to every major era of the Watchtower history."

> Some of the better-known publications of Jehovah's Witnesses include the word **watchtower** in their name. An early name of the organization was the Zion's Watchtower Tract Society, and the first magazine of the sect was called **The Watchtower**. That magazine is still published today. It is printed in 132 languages with a print run of 22 million copies per issue.

We listened with rapt attention as Paul continued his story. "As a Witness, I was raised in a hermetically sealed world. My life, my work, my friends, my family, and my culture were all tied to the organization. When I was nineteen, I applied to work at the worldwide headquarters in New York City. Much to my surprise, I was accepted and given a job working the night shift as freight elevator operator. I may not have had a glamorous job, but I had made it to headquarters, and I was the envy of those who knew me."

"What was your life like at headquarters?" Nellie Jo asked.

"Highly regimented would be an understatement," Paul reflected. "I spent three years of my life there. You were awakened at the same time every day. You ate at the same time in the same seat at the same table. And you were always subject to surveillance by other Witnesses. We were constantly encouraged to report anyone who violated one of the many prohibitions of the organization."

"Did you find any surprises at headquarters?" I inquired.

"Really," Paul responded, "the biggest surprise was the amount of drinking that took place at headquarters. We were allowed to consume alcohol in moderation, but some had different degrees of moderation than others. I literally drank every day when I was there. Jehovah's Witnesses have so many restrictions and taboos that the laxness of monitoring our drinking habits surprised me."

Jehovah's Witnesses must refrain from giving or receiving blood transfusions, using any kind of tobacco, celebrating birthdays and Christmas, observing Thanksgiving, saluting or pledging allegiance to the flag, and serving in the military.

We waited for Paul to continue his story. "When I returned to upstate New York after serving at headquarters," he said, "I went back to my work as a Pioneer, a Witness who gives at least a hundred hours a month going door to door. I had been doing door-to-door work for the Witnesses since I was five years old."

My research assistant, Russ, interjected, "What motivates a Jehovah's Witness to work so hard?"

Paul responded, "The organization fills you with a life of guilt. You can never do enough, so you keep pushing yourself to work harder and harder, hoping one day you will be worthy of living in Paradise on earth."

Paul paused for a moment. "I guess that guilt is the stick and Paradise is the carrot. Both really motivate Witnesses to go to homes and to 'give away' their literature for a donation. The organization is, in many ways, a publishing house disguised as a religion."

> *Jehovah's Witnesses sell millions of copies of their literature each month. They publish the New World Translation of the Holy Scriptures, their translation of the Bible; Watchtower and Awake magazines; and many books and brochures.*

The Doubts Begin

We were eager to hear how Paul began the journey away from Jehovah's Witnesses to Christianity, so he continued his story. "The hypocrisy at headquarters confused me and probably planted the first seeds of doubt. But I tried to hide those doubts with even more work for the organization.

"I married another third-generation Jehovah's Witness. She was a Special Pioneer since she gave 150 hours a month to door-to-door work. We soon moved from upstate New York to Texas and started attending a small Witness congregation."

Paul realized that he had to fill in some blanks for the three of us since we were not experts on Jehovah's Witnesses. "Each congregation is under the authority of the elders. The elders keep secret files on each member. If any wrongdoing takes place by a Witness, that act is noted in their file, and they will probably be brought before a tribunal for discipline. And Witnesses are encouraged to report any act of wrongdoing, such as smoking a cigarette, because failure to report it is a wrongdoing itself. A Witness is thus constantly living a life of both guilt and fear."

We could tell that Paul was taking us from this sidebar to his own story. We waited for him to explain. "I met a guy named Art at this Texas Kingdom Hall. He pulled me aside and asked me to meet him at his home. When I got there, he handed me a book called *Thirty Years a Watchtower Slave*. I dropped that book like it was a rattlesnake!" Paul laughed.

"You see," he explained, "we were prohibited from reading any of that kind of material. That's why the Internet is really hurting the organization today. Witnesses can look at that stuff online at night in the privacy of their homes. But the Internet wasn't available back then."

Nellie Jo didn't want Paul to get sidetracked. "What happened next?" she asked.

"I took it home and read it," he said. "I brought my wife, Patricia, into it and we both started reading the book and looking at old Witness literature. We started seeing, along with Art and his wife, the contradictions and the false prophecies."

Paul had been speaking so much to this point that his mouth was dry. He got some water and resumed his story. "The Witness organization," he said with emphasis, "is like a house of cards. If you start examining one false prophecy or one false doctrine, the whole deck begins to fall. That's what was happening to my wife and me."

> Jehovah's Witnesses believe there is one God—Jehovah—and that is the only correct name for God. For them Jesus is not the Son of God but Michael the archangel, the first of God's creations. When Michael came to earth, he took for himself the name Jesus. After his resurrection and return to heaven, Jesus resumed the name Michael. For Witnesses the Holy Spirit is not God; he is more of an active force rather than a person.

The more Paul and his wife studied, the more they began to doubt Witness doctrine. "Art introduced me to the New American Standard Bible," Paul smiled. "Any Bible other than the *New World Translation* was a big no-no. Not too much later, things began to fall apart in our lives. It started when my mother and father came to our home one evening."

The Cost of Disobedience

Paul's father noticed the old Jehovah's Witnesses' books on his table. "He asked me why I was reading the old material since we had new light. New light means that we have new revelation and that past prophecies and the words of past prophets are no longer valid. It appears to be the Witnesses' way of covering up what may be false prophecies of the past.

"Well, I told my father that I was struggling with some of the Witnesses' teaching, so I was trying to figure it all out. He went ballistic. He yelled at me, 'You've never been the same since you returned from headquarters!' And then he turned my wife and me in to the elders."

I looked at Paul's face. An event that took place years ago still marked his expression with pain. Confronted with their misdeeds before the elders, Paul and his wife broke emotionally. They cried and cried and promised they would not stray again.

"I know it might seem weird to you that we just didn't walk away from this mind-control game," Paul noted perceptively. "But once you become a Jehovah's Witness, they become your whole world. All of your relationships, friendships, family, and activities are tied up in the organization. It is extremely difficult to walk away."

A few months after this trauma, Paul had the opportunity to relocate to another town in Texas. Sensing that Jehovah was giving them an opportunity to start fresh, the couple made the move. But the file full of their misdeeds traveled to the Kingdom Hall in their new town.

"The whole scene just repeated itself," Paul reflected. "We had to go before this new group of elders while they ranted about our wrongdoings. Even though we had recanted for all that we had done, they found it necessary to put us through that same abuse all over again." Paul paused for a moment and took a breath. "And this is where things really started getting bad."

A Baby Is Born . . . a Baby Is Left to Die

Paul's wife soon gave birth to a daughter, their third child, whom they named Jenny. Patricia was cutting Jenny's fingernails one evening when she accidentally cut the baby's finger. Jenny started bleeding, and the bleeding would not stop. Paul and Patricia took her to a doctor, and he could not stop the bleeding either. So the five-week-old baby was rushed to the pediatric intensive care unit at the Santa Rosa Medical Center in San Antonio.

Paul and Patricia were anticipating the news that the doctor was about to give them. Nevertheless, his words hit them forcefully. "If your daughter does not have a blood transfusion, she will have either brain damage or heart failure and die," the doctor said gently. "You only have twelve hours to decide."

The Jehovah's Witnesses couple were torn as they had never been before. The organization had misinterpreted biblical texts in Leviticus and Acts that dealt with blood from animal sacrifices. They concluded that no Witness could accept or receive a blood transfusion.

"My wife and I thought that Jehovah was testing us because we questioned the organization," Paul recalled sadly. "You talk about guilt. Tremendous guilt." Paul paused.

I had a lump in my throat. I could sense the deep emotions in Nellie Jo and Russ as well.

"We met with the doctor," Paul said slowly. "We told him, 'We are going to let her die.'"

Even though the event took place several years ago, I wanted to scream, "No! Don't let it happen!"

The doctor did not accept the response the Blizards gave him. The hospital management got a judge out of bed. The judge gave a court order to proceed with the transfusion. Paul and Patricia were charged with child abuse and neglect. The media jumped on the story. Things were spiraling out of control in their lives.

Elders from the congregation came to the hospital and urged Paul to take Jenny from the hospital bed before she had the transfusion. Paul refused. He argued that he had been obedient to the Witness doctrine, that the legal system was calling the shots. The elder responded maliciously, "I hope your daughter gets hepatitis from the blood."

"We watched the transfusion take place," Paul told us. "We felt awful."

Jenny survived this ordeal, but Paul and Patricia would learn that the baby had a terminal liver disease. She had a life expectancy of six to seven years.

"Throughout this entire trial," Paul said, "I kept thinking the same thought. The Jehovah's Witnesses would have let my daughter die. Can you imagine feeling guilty that your child is alive?"

Another Knock on the Door

Some time later, Paul heard a knock on his door at home. The woman standing at the door said, "I'm your neighbor. I heard you had a sick child. I wanted to make you a meal."

Paul recalls that moment. "She had a pan of chicken. I just looked at her and couldn't believe what she was saying and doing. The Witnesses, who were supposed to be my family, were treating us like scum. And here was this woman who didn't even know us, showing love and concern. I had never experienced anything like this before. I had never seen this type of love before."

Paul reflected, "I had argued hundreds of times with Christians and pastors. I hardly ever lost an argument when I went door to door as a Witness. I could tie Christians in doctrinal pretzels. I could tear down the concept of the Trinity, the celebration of Christmas, and serving in the military. But when that woman came to my home, I could not proof text against Christian love."

I thought about Paul's words. I cannot count the times I have invited Jehovah's Witnesses into my home for the sole purpose of doctrinal debate. And while I will never apologize for taking a stand for truth, I cannot honestly say that I was demonstrating Christlike love toward the Witnesses. I have been more interested in winning debates than winning hearts. Paul's story was convicting me.

> The first three presidents of the Jehovah's Witnesses are the most important names in the relatively brief history of the movement. Charles T. Russell was the founder. His prediction of the beginning of the Millennium in 1914 was the impetus that caused many to follow this new sect. Russell died in 1916 and was succeeded by Joseph Franklin "Judge" Rutherford. He was the doctrinal writer for the Witnesses, averaging one new book each year. Rutherford also reinforced the emphasis on door-to-door witnessing. Nathan Knorr followed Rutherford in 1942. Knorr led a great missionary movement, including the establishment of a training school to prepare Witnesses for a worldwide missionary thrust. Under Knorr's leadership, Witnesses grew from 115,000 to more than 2 million.

Paul continued. "I couldn't deal with this Christian love," he said. "A prayer group from this lady's church started bringing meals on a regular basis. They started praying for us. That love drove me back to the banned New American Standard Bible. I had to learn what this was all about."

Paul also started meeting with the pastor of that church in secret. "He didn't pull his apologetics books off the shelf to show me the errors of Witness theology. He was very kind. When I would ask him a question, he would say, 'Let's see what the Bible says about that.'"

Finally . . . a Real Witness

"I cannot describe the internal turmoil my wife and I were experiencing," Paul told us. "I told my wife that we needed to get away, so we drove to San Angelo. While we were in a mall, we saw a

Christian bookstore. We decided to go in. We felt like we were on some undercover mission sneaking around."

After looking at some books, Paul decided to approach a woman at the register. "Look," he said, "I am really confused. My wife and I are Jehovah's Witnesses. We don't know what to do."

The woman listened to Paul for a few minutes and then declared, "You just need to give your heart to Jesus." Paul looked at her and said, "What?" She responded, "You need to get saved."

This woman explained the gospel. She told Paul and Patricia about repentance of sins, of salvation by grace not by works, about the promise of forgiveness and the hope of eternal life for all those who believe. She explained a gospel that removed guilt, not a religion that burdened people with guilt.

> In the beliefs of Jehovah's Witnesses, there is no salvation through Jesus Christ, since Jesus is not God but Michael the archangel. Salvation is thus not based on relationship with Jesus Christ, but on faithfulness and strict obedience to the multitude of requirements of the Witnesses. Therefore a Witness cannot declare to be saved; the Witness can only hope that his or her obedience is enough to get to Paradise.

"On the way home," Paul reflected, "I pulled the car over onto the side of the road so we could talk. On that day in 1982, one lost person told another lost person how to be saved. We gave our lives to Christ."

Paul's next several words were convicting. "I had knocked on doors for twenty-eight years," he told us. "I have been in thousands of homes of Christians, including pastors. I have had doors slammed in my face, dogs sicked on me, and water thrown on me. But I never, never, never had anyone share the gospel with me. No one, that is, except a clerk in a Christian bookstore."

Nellie Jo asked Paul, "What did you feel like after you accepted Christ?"

Paul responded, "I felt like a legion of demons had left me. I felt like the biggest burden of my life had been lifted. I felt like I finally had the hope and assurance of eternity."

> *Witnesses believe in an afterlife. There will be an elite group of 144,000 who actually go to heaven. The rest of the Jehovah's Witnesses will live on the new earth established in the Millennium. Everyone else will be annihilated or disappear after death. For the Witnesses there is no hell.*

"My wife and I went to a First Baptist Church that Sunday. The pastor saw me and was amazed that I was there in public. At the time of invitation, we declared to the church that we had accepted Christ. It was quite a day," Paul said with a smile.

"The very next day the elders from the Kingdom Hall called," Paul told us. "They were very upset that we had joined a Baptist church. They told me that they were having an emergency-called judicial committee meeting to hear my case. It was a big tribunal. They demanded my presence."

Paul recalled how upset he was. "I just starting pacing and getting all upset. Then the doorbell rang. The pastor said that he just sensed he needed to come by and see if I needed anything. I told him about the meeting the next day. He could tell how upset I was.

"Then he made a simple suggestion. He said, 'Tell them you're not coming.'

"'Say what?' I responded.

"He said, 'Paul, you are no longer under their control or authority. You don't have to go. Call them.'"

Paul smiled at us. "That's what I did. I just called the elder and told him I wouldn't be there. He screamed and told me I had to be there. I told him I was no longer a part of his program. I was a child of God. And I hung up and had the biggest smile on my face."

The Aftermath

The next day Paul and Patricia Blizard were disfellowshiped from the Jehovah's Witnesses. The charge was "conduct unbecoming a Christian." All Witnesses were to cease having any contact with the Blizards, including Paul and Patricia's family.

Jenny died at age six and a half. None of her grandparents or any of her Witness family came to the funeral. But more than four hundred of Paul and Patricia's new family were there. The Christians were there in force.

To this day, Paul has not heard from any of his family. He has not heard a word since 1982. The cost of following Christ has not been small.

What Now?

It was not easy for me to hold back tears. I cannot imagine bearing the cost that Paul and Patricia did. I cannot imagine losing a child. I cannot imagine never hearing from my entire family. But the Blizards found Christ, and they will tell you in a moment's notice that the cost has been worth the gain.

"Paul," I asked, "what can you say to those who will read your story? What can you tell Christians about reaching Jehovah's Witnesses today?"

"The woman who brought the pan of chicken did more to change my attitude toward Christians than any preacher I had ever met," he told us. "That one act of kindness pushed me over the edge."

Then he reminded us of the Christian bookstore clerk who was bold with her witness at just the right time. God had arranged an appointment for the Blizards with one who was obedient to share the gospel.

Finally, Paul reminded us how his examination of the documents of Jehovah's Witnesses created an internal dissonance that prompted him to search further for truth. "If you can get them to look honestly at the prophecies of their leaders over the history of the movement, they will have to admit that something is wrong," he said.

Today, as a Baptist pastor, Paul Blizard also has a ministry to ex-Jehovah's Witnesses. "Most of these ex-Witnesses are not Christians," he told us. "Many of them are having a very difficult time adjusting to the isolation that leaving the organization brings. I try to encourage them so that I might have the opportunity to share the gospel of Christ with them."

———oᴤ₿◊ᴏ———

It had been two months since my last *Unexpected Journey* interview. But the wait had been worth it. We had heard the inspiring story of one man who had broken the shackles of a false religion and found the love of the one true God in Jesus Christ. Even to this day, Paul Blizard counts the cost of being a Christian. But in the midst of the trials he endures, he counts it all joy.

Nellie Jo, Russ, and I got our items together. I left my cell phone in Paul's office, so Russ went back into the building to get it for me. When he returned to the car, we all said a collective "Wow!" The return trip would be a time of reflection, commitment, and joy. We would not forget this meeting.

This time we would not have to wait two months to continue our own journey. In just ten days we would be in two more states doing back-to-back interviews. The first would be the story of an agnostic, someone who had doubts about the existence of God. The second would be a breathtaking interview with an ex-witch. I am not certain what you, the reader, are expecting in these next chapters, but I am quite certain you will be surprised by what you read.

CHAPTER SIX

"THERE ARE SO MANY PEOPLE JUST LIKE ME"

A FORMER AGNOSTIC TELLS HER STORY

August 19
Greer, South Carolina

My wife and I thrive in a warm environment. Our idea of a cold spell is when the temperature dips below eighty degrees. We were therefore in our element for the next two days and the next two *Unexpected Journey* interviews. Our flight took us into the Greenville/Spartanburg airport in South Carolina. From there we would drive to Greer, just a few miles from the airport, and then into nearby North Carolina.

A bank time and temperature sign told us the temperature had climbed to ninety-three degrees. The humidity made it feel even hotter. We loved it.

We drove to a newly developed area in Greer, a town about equal distance between the two larger cities of Greenville and Spartanburg. The subdivision could not have been too old, because construction was still taking place in the area. After a few turns, we found ourselves at the very neat home of Jeff and Mia Hughey. Our appointment was with Mia.

Not Your Typical Housewife

I guess I am sometimes guilty of stereotyping. When we were greeted by the twentysomething woman (she would later tell us that her age was twenty-nine), I thought that this interview might be a bit dull. We were in a lovely and neat suburban home. The house smelled of fresh baking (cookies were on the way), and Mia was neatly dressed, greeting us with a smile. *Certainly we won't hear much of anything interesting from this young suburban mom,* I thought. I would soon find out that I thought wrong.

After Nellie Jo and I set up the recording equipment at a breakfast table, Mia told us that she was a fairly new Christian. She also shared with us that a Mormon family lived on the same street as she did. "They really tempted me to join them, with their family values and all," she commented. "I'm glad I found the truth instead."

Mia began by telling us she had a son and a daughter, both preschoolers. And then she questioned why we would be interested in her story. "You are interviewing Mormons, Buddhists, witches, and satanists," she said. "My story is pretty boring in comparison." For a moment I feared that she might be right. And that is when we started hearing her story.

"I was the only child of two partying hippies," she began. Okay, first stereotype shattered. "And my mom was someone who made fun of the name of Jesus," she added. Another preconceived notion gone. "I started drinking and partying when I was eleven years old." By this time I realized that the pretty housewife we were interviewing was not your typical soccer mom.

Turning against the Church

"Let's back up," I said to Mia. "Tell us about your parents."

She responded, "Mom and Dad were your classic Vietnam-era hippies. I grew up the first nine years of my life in a house where constant partying was commonplace.

"Eventually my parents got a divorce, and I moved with my mother when I was nine years old. She brought me to see my father a few times, but his living conditions were really bad," she said matter-of-factly. "She didn't want me to be subjected to his lifestyle.

"So my mom is now a single parent trying to raise a kid on her own. She gets a job at a bank and has to grow up pretty quickly.

"Mom had taken me to church when I was five years old. She thought it was good for me to go to church; I'm not sure why. Well, we started attending this church, and a bunch of men in suits ushered me into an office. They started asking me a bunch of questions. One of them asked me if I believed Jesus was my Savior. I was scared, so I just said yes. They all started crying. I didn't have a clue what they had been talking about, and their crying just freaked me out."

When Mia's mother found out what had happened, she took her daughter out of the church. Mia's mother became disillusioned with organized religion because of this event. She started mocking churchgoers and making fun of the name of Jesus. Mia's early childhood environment was filled with animosity against Christians and church. The young girl did not choose to be an agnostic. She simply was raised in a home that created significant doubt about the reality of God.

No Parents, No God, No Boundaries

Mia's mother was often too busy to provide her daughter the oversight and guidance she felt she needed. She would leave her child alone occasionally, when Mia was as young as eleven years old, to attend classes and seminars. "Mom had it tough too," Mia shared with us. "She was not a Christian, and she was trying to find her own way. And she was trying to support the two of us; she went out of town to the classes to better herself so she could make more money.

"My mother had this false image of me," Mia told us. "Because I made good grades and seemed mature for my age, she trusted me totally. Little did she know that when she left me alone, the partying began. It is a miracle I made it to where I am today. I had no parents looking after me, no concept of God, and no boundaries. I had no anchor in my life."

> In its simplest terms, agnosticism is the belief that God's existence cannot be known for certain. An agnostic is a person who says that God's existence can neither be proved nor disproved on the basis of current evidence.

That is the reason Mia began a relationship with "an abusive jerk who was older than me." She described her broken condition. "When you are a lost and lonely child with no boundaries, you're going to run to anything that comes your way with open arms." The first person she ran to was a boy who treated her terribly. "I spent a very critical time in my life with this horrible guy," she recalled painfully.

"I felt like I was an inconvenience to my mother. I felt like I was the result of a big mistake of her relationship with my father, whom she seemed to hate. I had no one. My self-esteem was so low. Looking back, I can't believe I put up with that creep. I just didn't think I deserved anyone better."

Speaking of her lack of religious faith, Mia commented, "If I had known to turn to God, I might not have had the awful childhood I had. But my mother turned me off to God and Jesus. I didn't consider religion an option."

> An atheist believes with certainty that no God or gods exist. But an agnostic usually holds the question of God's existence open if reliable evidence becomes available. Still some other agnostics do not even think about such issues. At least from a superficial perspective, the existence of God is not something they think about.

Mia did attend vacation Bible school at a church once when she was very young. "I didn't learn anything about Jesus, but I sure had fun with the activities and crafts. And we did have to memorize John 3:16, but no one explained it to us. I wonder if my life would have changed if someone had taken time to talk with me about Jesus," she said wistfully.

The pause in her reflections was interrupted when her husband Jeff walked into the house. We were introduced to Jeff, a warm and friendly man who welcomed us into his home. I offered for Jeff to join us for the interview, but he declined. He had some more work to do before they left for the beaches of Destin, Florida, the next day.

The mention of Destin and beaches started a ten-minute conversation that left my Nellie Jo and me anticipating our own next trip to the beach. Jeff left, and we continued the conversation with his wife.

From Bad Relationship to Worse Lifestyle

"I don't remember how I got the courage to leave the monster I was dating, but I finally did. He threatened to kill me if I ever left him, so I carried a club with me for the next two years," Mia recalled. "I guess I felt like I could leave him because I had started making new friends."

Nellie Jo asked about her new friends. "Well, they were pot-smoking, drug-taking, bar-hopping friends. I was only fifteen, and they were older, but I looked much older than my age then," she reflected. "I never got carded in a bar even one time in downtown Knoxville. I would wear black clothes, a tight miniskirt, fishnet hose, and combat boots. I would make my face real white to contrast with the clothes, and I would wear bright red lipstick. The gothic look was in, so I tried it for a while."

The image of this suburban housewife dressed in that attire went beyond my imagination. Then Mia spoke some profound words. "When you have no God and no parents, you are begging for someone to accept you," she told us. "I got attention from this group. I fit in. I thought I had found the answer."

She paused for a moment and took a breath. "I was hurting so much then," she said softly. "I stayed depressed. Life was so painful; it was raw human suffering. I hurt so much on the inside. Suicide was a constant part of my thought patterns. Oh, how I needed God then."

But Mia's life did not include God. So she turned to a tough group of older teenagers for acceptance. "The girls in this group introduced me to drugs," she remembered. "I remember the first time I took some. I laughed for six or seven hours. I couldn't remember the last time I had laughed. I only knew depression. But now I was laughing, free from pain and free from my abusive boyfriend. I felt great, at least for a little while."

A Restless Teenager

Mia left that group when she met a new boyfriend. "He was really a sweet guy. He came from a Christian home, but I never heard him talk about his religion. Instead, I introduced him to drugs. I stayed with him about two years," she said. "I then moved on again."

I noted to Mia her restlessness as a youth. "You've got that right," she affirmed. "I was seeking someone to accept me, but I didn't feel like I deserved acceptance. So I kept moving from one thing to another."

She mused that some of those tendencies are still with her today. "You know," she began, "even though I am a Christian now, I still have the wanderlust spirit. My dream, my big dream when I was younger, was to buy a used Volkswagen van and travel all over the United States. I could work odd jobs, shower at truck stops, and sleep in the van. I told Jeff that I wanted to do that when the kids are grown. You should have seen the look on his face! He is a real homebody."

I commented that, despite my demanding travel schedule, I was a homebody at heart. But Nellie Jo's spirit resonated with Mia's. My wife loves traveling with me now that our boys are grown.

As we returned to Mia's story, we learned that her life was about to take another significant turn. Her mother had remarried. Mia and her new stepfather just did not get along. "And when I was eighteen," she said with sadness, "they told me I had thirty days to leave the house. They did not like the hours I kept and the noise my boyfriend's car made. We were waking up *their* baby." She emphasized 'their' to show that she felt that she was not a part of this new family.

{ *Since no official records are kept on agnostics, it is difficult to know how many agnostics there are in the United States. Most data lump together agnostics, atheists, and skeptics. A rough estimate of the agnostic population in America would be about 1 million.*

"I had to move to a place I called the crack house," she told us. "It was awful. There was dirt and cockroaches everywhere. But I could afford the monthly rent of two hundred dollars, and I was making good money in the bar where I worked. There was the mentally imbalanced guy that lived on my hallway in this former World War II dormitory. He would wait up for me every night, even when I got in at four in the morning. I think God was looking after me so that nothing bad happened to me while I lived there."

A Reunion with Her Father

By this point in the interview, Nellie Jo and I could see clearly the pattern Mia was communicating to us. She had no one she could call family. She had no God in whom she could place her trust and dependence. And she was trying to fill the huge void in her life with bad relationships, drugs, and alcohol.

Mia began using drugs more often. "That was the sum of my life. Work in the bar until the early morning hours. Get drunk and do drugs. Then go to my room in the crack house and sleep all day."

She then would make yet another move in her life. "One day the rent was due and I had no money. I had spent it all on drugs. But I didn't want to go back to the bar where I worked. My boss was a real creep. So I called my father. It was really strange. I had not seen him in years. It was really strange."

She continued, "My dad was a big partyer. But I still had some good memories of him. How he loved me. How he used to watch cartoons with me when I was little. When I told him of my problem, he asked me to come live with him. He even told me I didn't have to work. I had been working two jobs since I was a young teenager."

Mia made the immediate decision to move in with her father. "I knew I was on a downward spiral and needed help," she said. She drove to Morristown, Tennessee, to his mobile home. "I didn't know what to call him," she recalled. 'Daddy' just didn't work anymore. I couldn't call him Fred either. So for a couple of weeks I didn't call him anything."

Some pundits have devised subcategories of agnostics:

- *Agnostic theists believe that a deity probably exists; they just are not certain.*
- *Agnostic atheists believe that it is improbable that a deity exists; but they are not certain either.*
- *Agnostic humanists are uncertain about the existence of God, and they really do believe the issue to be important. They subscribe to ethical and moral codes from secular sources.*

One day Mia's father asked her if she wanted to go for a ride with him in his truck. They went from one rural bar to another. "We call them honkytonks in East Tennessee," she laughed. "He was amazed that his little girl could match him drinking beer for beer. On the way home we split another six-pack of beer and just talked and talked. Before that night was over, I called him 'Daddy.'"

Mia noticed that Nellie Jo had goose bumps on her arm. She asked my wife if she was cold. Nellie Jo responded, "No, not at all. Your story is giving me goose bumps."

"We continued to hang out in these country bars," Mia shared with us. "You may not understand, but I was desperate for family. Daddy introduced me to his buddies, Vietnam vets. I started spending time with them at this one bar that was their gathering spot. I got to know them. It was a place that most Christians would never go near. But I began to love those old men. Those big, burly, dirty men became my family. And they treated me with love and respect."

Mia continued her reflections on this era of her life. "I think if Christians could understand that there are a lot of people like me out there, they could make a big difference. I didn't know if God existed, but I did know that something was missing in my life. If only a true Christian had befriended me . . ."

Mia returned to her story. "I started tending bar a couple of nights a week in the bar where Daddy and his buddies hung out," she recalled. Most of them were Vietnam vets, and a few served in World War II. Cecil was one of those World War II vets. He was the sweetest, most precious man you could ever know. The jukebox played oldies from the 50s, 60s, and 70s. We would drink and sing at the top of our lungs and even dance."

The love that Mia had for these men was obvious in our conversation with her. I am not certain if this written word communicates well the passion with which she spoke when she talked to us about them.

"My friends were all old men. I had never been so loved and so accepted," she said tearfully. "I had never been truly loved by a man, and now I had total love and total acceptance by guys who were like fathers to me. I felt like I had come home. Rejection had defined my life, and now I felt like I had finally been accepted."

And Then Comes Marriage

Mia continued to work in the bar some at night and in a convenience store during the day. One day an old friend from elementary school walked into the store, and the two women recognized each other. "My friend invited me to a party. I did not have many friends my own age, so I was ready to go," she told us.

"Well, I was never shy," she said, "and I was always ready to party. Three other girls and I were smoking pot in a car when Jeff, my future husband, walks up to the car. I offered him some pot, but he refused. He said he didn't do that, even if it made him seen uncool. But he was drinking moonshine."

The next few lines are accompanied by a broad smile and a twinkle in her eyes. "I was repulsed, not interested in Jeff," she said. "I was drawn to long-haired losers, and here comes this short-haired, preppy jock to the car.

"The next thing I know, all the girls have left but me, and Jeff is driving the car," she mused. "I have no idea how that happened. Well, he gets lost, and I tell him to get me back to the party right then. He was very much the gentleman; he said he just wanted to get to know me a little. It took forever, but we made it back.

"During the night, Jeff asked me for my phone number. I gave it to him; I didn't think anything about it because I always gave my number if a guy asked. I was a lonely and lost girl looking and hoping for love."

Mia was shocked when Jeff called the next day. "Now get this," she said emphatically. "Jeff calls to apologize for his behavior last night. I was blown away. I had guys smash me in the face and not apologize."

> Agnostic comes from two Greek words. A is a prefix that negates a word. It can literally be translated "not." Gnosis means "knowledge" or "knowing." Agnostic thus literally means "not knowing." Agnostics do not know if God exists or not.

Eventually Jeff and Mia started dating. The early relationship was rocky. "I was so insecure," Mia reminded us. "I couldn't understand why this clean-cut guy from a middle-class family wanted to have anything to do with me. But the dating relationship survived, and about a year later Jeff proposed to me."

God Is Back in the Picture

Mia never really was an ardent advocate of the agnostic position. You can search the Internet for the word *agnosticism* and find many individuals and groups that fiercely defend their position that the existence of God cannot be known. To use an oxymoron, they are "agnostic evangelists."

But Mia was never a firebrand for her beliefs. While quietly doubting the reality of God, she went about her life seemingly more concerned about more pressing matters. I suspect that the majority of agnostics in America are more like Mia than the firebrands.

Still, Mia's agnostic beliefs would surface from time to time. She recalls an argument her fiancé, Jeff, had with a friend who was an atheist. "I found myself pulling for the atheist," Mia said with a smile. "When he would make a point, I would say, 'Yeah, that's what I believe.' But Jeff kept pressing this guy. Like when the atheistic friend said that humanity was created by evolutionary forces, Jeff would ask him where the evolutionary forces came from. Jeff kept pushing him to say where the beginning of everything was. The guy finally gave in and said, 'I guess it must be God.' Those words hit me hard; I couldn't get them out of my mind."

God seemed to be the relentless pursuer of Mia. "After Jeff proposed to me," she said, "I started looking for a church to have the wedding in. I know that sounds weird—an agnostic looking for a church—but I was really interested in a beautiful church building."

She chose a Presbyterian church that she and her mother had attended when Mia was a child. "It is such a beautiful place. The stained-glass windows are incredible. I knew that was the place. But you had to be a member of the church to get married there. So I started visiting and soon told the pastor that I wanted to join. I became a member of that church without anyone asking me any questions about my relationship with God."

When Mia was attending that church, however, she felt deep and inexplicable emotions. "I would just start crying for no reason," she recalls. "I had no idea that the Holy Spirit was working in my life. I felt a comfortable closeness and trust with the pastor, maybe because he was a Vietnam vet. I did learn there that church was an okay place to be."

> *Thomas H. Huxley is credited with coining the term agnosticism in 1876. His definition of the term was that an agnostic is someone who believes that we do not and cannot know for certain if God exists.*

From Motherhood to Christianity

After Jeff and Mia were married, they moved to Greenville, South Carolina, where Jeff had been offered a job. "I resented him for that," Mia told us. "The greatest security I had in the world was my Daddy and his drinking buddies. Jeff took me away from the people I had come to know and love. I hated the 'big city.' I hated my home. I hated my job."

Mia and a friend started drinking almost every day after work. "That's all I had to look forward to. The highlight of my life was getting passing-out drunk," she said sadly.

Then Mia learned that she was pregnant.

"Everything changed. I immediately stopped drinking and smoking. Having a baby was the dream of my life. I knew if I had this child, he would love me and accept me unconditionally. I wanted someone I could love with all my heart without fear of being hurt."

I swallowed hard as I heard her testimony. I looked around at the neat house. I saw the photographs of family members. No outsider ever could have guessed the pain that was once so constant in Mia's life.

A son was born in September 1999. "I remember thinking that if there was a God, he would take my baby from me. I had been so terrible that if God did exist, he would surely punish me for my life. I found myself staying up all night sometimes, watching my baby sleep, just to make sure he was okay."

Three years later Mia gave birth to a daughter. "Now I had two kids," she said, "and I had to make sure they had everything I didn't have as a child. I wanted them as far away from my child-hood as possible. I wanted them to have Jeff's *Leave It to Beaver* childhood."

Nellie Jo and I both laughed at her description. "I told Jeff we needed to get the kids in a church. That must have really weirded him out," she told us. "But I knew other kids had a great time in churches. I had heard about church camps and activities, and I wanted that for my children."

This time Mia relented to Jeff's urging to go to a Baptist church, which was his background and childhood. The first Baptist church was a big turnoff to Mia. "The preacher kept shouting 'Jesus, Jesus, Jesus.' I found myself mocking him like my mother used to do."

But Mia persisted and found a church in nearby Taylors that she thought was great for her children. "They had so many things for children," Mia recalled. She was not yet aware of her own divine appointment at the church.

In the meantime, Mia's mother began visiting Mia and the children.

One Sunday Mia's mother went to church with her. Mia feared how her mother would respond. She still had clear memories of her mother mocking the name of Jesus.

"I guess by this time I was a seeker agnostic," Mia explained. "I was still uncertain about the existence of God, but I had a lot of questions. My mom and I went to Sunday school and worship together. The Sunday school teacher was a lawyer with a military background. He said he had decided to skip the originally planned lesson. Instead, he gave an incredible lesson on the exis-tence of God."

Mia was stunned. She sensed that God had prepared that teacher and that class just for her. "I asked a lot of questions," she continued. "And I was afraid to ask them because I didn't want people to know I did not fully accept the existence of God. But he answered every question perfectly. I burst into tears as I was getting ready to go into the worship service."

When the service began, the congregation sang one of the few hymns that Mia knew, "Amazing Grace." Between the Sunday school class and the music, Mia finally understood. She asked Jesus to be her Savior. The church had a public invitation, and she moved toward the counselors to share her decision.

Afterward, Mia had to face her mother, that same mother who had mocked the name of Jesus. What would she say to her daughter who was now a follower of Christ?

Mia's mother spoke first: "I accepted Christ the same time you did." Mia was stunned. Mother and daughter wept together. And on that warm summer day in 2003, they both finally found the Father who loved and accepted them unconditionally.

"I really needed the affirmation of my mom," Mia said softly. She needed to hear from the mother who had been so influential in her rejection of God.

"I believe every agnostic and atheist is just a lost soul seeking love," Mia told us. "Never give up on a person. Never judge them. Accept them as they are. And soon they will see Christ in you."

———✦———

Nellie Jo and I hugged our new friend as we left her home. The sky was a bright blue, and the sunshine brought waves of warmth. But we had felt even greater warmth in Mia's home. The love of Christ was so clearly evident in the life of this young woman who, just months earlier, did not even know if God existed. God is good. God is so very good.

The next trip would only take three hours by car as we headed for Greensboro, North Carolina. An ex-witch named Kathi would be waiting for us. We were about to hear yet another amazing story.

CHAPTER SEVEN

"I BECAME ADEPT AT CASTING SPELLS"

THE AMAZING TESTIMONY OF A FORMER WITCH

August 21
Greensboro, North Carolina

Our previous interview with Mia had been very encouraging. The drive from Greer, South Carolina, to Greensboro, North Carolina, took place on a sun-drenched day. My wife and I were in a good mood indeed. Our travels had left us with little time for sleep, but on this day we would arrive at our hotel in the early evening. A good night's sleep awaited us. Everything seemed to be going our way.

When we awoke the next morning, Nellie Jo and I were talking with excited anticipation. She told me she had never met a former witch. I told her I had never met a witch or a former witch. My wife gave me the look.

We thought we left the hotel in plenty of time for our 10:00 a.m. meeting with Kathi Sharpe. But once again my direction-deficient mind kept missing our destination. I called Kathi, who cheerfully guided me by cell phone to the Bob Evans restaurant that I must have passed four times. At least I asked for directions!

Meeting an Ex-Witch

I don't think I had a stereotypical image of what a former witch would look or act like. My initial reaction was that Kathi seemed "normal," whatever that means. Within a few hours I could no longer use the term *normal* to describe Kathi Sharpe. To the contrary, my wife and I both described her as extraordinary.

When I first proposed this *Unexpected Journey* project to Zondervan, my friend and editor Paul Engle suggested parameters for the book. Among his suggestions was that each chapter should contain the concise and powerful story of the interviewee. The book would not be a lengthy treatise on other faiths, nor would it be an extensive biographical account of each participant.

Like most of those we interviewed, the challenge of telling Kathi's story in a few pages was significant. I think you will agree with me by the time you get to the end of this chapter: this woman has a remarkable story that leaves you with a desire to hear more.

> *Wicca is the term that refers to a polytheistic (more than one god) neo-pagan nature religion that has as its central deity a mother goddess and that includes the use of herbal magick and divination. Adherents of this faith are often called "Wiccans," and sometimes they refer to themselves as "witches." "Magick" denotes paranormal and occultic activity in contrast to the entertaining legerdemain called "magic."*

A Childhood without God

The mid-morning crowd at Bob Evans was relatively small. The employees were happy for us to occupy a table for a few hours. The waitress brought our orders. My oatmeal loaded with brown sugar was the best I have ever tasted. Maybe I was just hungry.

After a few minutes of conversation with Kathi Sharpe, we knew we were hearing from a smart woman with a quick and sometimes mischievous wit. She told us at the onset of our conversation that she often brings witches to church. My imagination of that scenario made me smile.

We then asked Kathi to start at the beginning. We had learned this far in our *Unexpected Journey* project that childhood experiences often explain much of one's life direction. Kathi's story was no exception.

"By the time I was around ten years old," she began, "I had read the Bible through several times. I wasn't trying to be religious; I just read everything I could get my hands on." The town library had only a small number of volumes, and she had read them all as well. "Reading was my way of escape," she said.

Kathi had grown up in a small New England farming community where she had been influenced by a mishmash of family and local occultic folklore. She had also been involved in the Theta Rho and Rainbow Girls (The Oddfellows and Masonic girls' groups). She noted, "Most people have childhood 'filters' for the occult, but I kind of grew up with little bits and pieces of it on the periphery. Some of it was minor stuff, but I look back on other things and say, 'Wow!' That was real, solid occultic teaching I was getting back then without realizing it.

"My parents had no particular spiritual inclinations, but we did attend an ultraliberal Congregationalist church for a while," she recalled. "One time in Sunday school a teacher told us that the story of Jonah was just a myth, that whales could not swallow humans. I debated with the teacher and told her that the Bible did not say it was a whale; it said that a great fish swallowed Jonah. And then I proceeded to show her library books that showed this could happen. I was kicked out of the class. You have to realize, I didn't believe or care if Jonah had gone down the hatch or not. I was arguing because the teacher got it wrong, not because I believed in the authority of the Bible."

Kathi's church adventures did not end there. She started challenging the preacher of the small church during his sermons. "I knew the Bible better than he did," Kathi said without boasting. "Not because I'd studied, not because I believed, but just through superficial reading.

"He basically said that all religions were the same," she continued. "But it was easy to see that the Bible said differently. Unfortunately, what I *didn't* see was the big picture of salvation ... something that I never heard preached there. Eventually they asked my parents not to bring me to church because I asked too many questions."

The family moved and attended a church in the same denomination. While relationships were less contentious there, the pastor was not much more knowledgeable about the Bible than the minister at the first church. Kathi still heard no message of salvation.

Kathi feels that her childhood experiences influenced the paths she would later take. "I was so mad at the preacher. I was mad at my parents. I couldn't understand why we were attending a church where *nothing* was believed. If my parents had just taken me to a vacation Bible school where the Word was taught, or if I had encountered anyone who would tell me the truth of the gospel, then I might never have veered off the way I did."

The waitress came by again to see if we needed anything. The interruption allowed us to move to another era of Kathi's life.

A Runaway Teen and Multiple Problems

"My relationship with my parents deteriorated as I moved into my early teen years," Kathi resumed. "We argued continuously. At fifteen I ran away from home. But because it was illegal in the state for a minor to run away, my parents pressed charges. I became even more rebellious."

During this time of conflict and rebellion, Kathi met an older man who seemed to offer her a refuge from her problems. "He totally charmed me," she said. "Later I would learn what type of person he was. The treatment was awful. And this man claimed to be a Christian." The two of them visited several churches during their time together, sometimes for services or financial help. "During this time I became very jaded against Christianity," she said.

One of the churches they visited was a Mormon church. "But I could tell they were way off from what the Bible said," she reflected. "Again, I didn't know or care about the Bible's authority; I just knew they were wrong from a plain reading of what the book had to say."

When Kathi turned eighteen, the man kicked her out of the house. "He didn't want an adult," she explained. "I was shattered. I thought that despite the way he treated me he loved me. I slept in an assortment of places: the homeless shelter, the streets, and a job site for day laborers. At that last place, I was raped and became pregnant. I was afraid to press charges."

Her tragic journey continued. "I left the state and met a guy I had known in high school. We got married. He also said he was a Christian. I gave birth to my son, one of the beautiful blessings in my awful life. My husband, this so-called Christian, treated me terribly. I then got pregnant a second time. I left him after he refused to change. I would later give birth to a beautiful daughter."

Kathi related one other story about her husband. "Despite the fact that I had told him never to come to the house, he showed up anyway. He had this weird dude with him. He claimed to be a preacher. This preacher told me that my husband had every right to treat me like he did because the Bible said so. I chased both of them out of the house."

I wish I could have seen that confrontation.

"So," I said to Kathi, "your experience with those claiming to be Christians included liberals who believed in nothing, wife abusers, and nuts."

"You got it," she replied. "I was staying as far away from Christians as I could."

The Pilgrimage to Witchcraft

Kathi continued, "I had already been doing some explorations into paganism, though I didn't know then what it was called. I still loved books and reading and continued to look at every book I could get my hands on—including books on ancient cultures.

"One day while I was pregnant with my daughter, I found a book on goddesses. I thought, 'It would be neat to worship them.' See, I knew that I was lacking something, and I was reaching out spiritually. I began to make up little prayers and offerings to these goddesses completely on my own. What I was doing was not based on history or fact, just on what I felt. My explorations at that point were not based on any power relationship with these entities and really did not resemble Wicca or paganism very much."

> Christians often use the word **paganism** erroneously to refer any person who is not a Christian. The meaning of **pagan** is one whose religious beliefs are earth- or nature-centered, most often including the worship of one or more goddesses. Wicca is one form of paganism.

Kathi's story continued. "After my daughter was born, I moved to another state and began living in a bizarre relationship. I was young, had two kids, no real emotional support, and no money or skills. I made a new friend and started watching her kids. I was attracted to her extensive bookshelves. She had all these books on spirituality, including many on goddesses, worship, magick, paganism, and witchcraft.

"I asked my new friend about her books, and she rather calmly said, 'Oh yeah, I'm a witch.' She began to teach me many things, including rituals and spells. She had a very informal, almost casual, approach to religion. In a way witchcraft had always been presented to me as evil and sinister. But what my friend taught me seemed quite the opposite. It was not at all what I'd heard in church and seen in the movies. I was taught that the goddess and the power within Wicca were beneficial and that one must *never* harm another."

> The main tenet of Wicca is called the "Wiccan Rede." It states, "An it harm none, do as ye will." Essentially it means you can do anything as long as you don't hurt someone else. But views of what causes harm can vary from person to person.

Kathi thought this new power, this magick (a word often used by adherents to distinguish the occultic and paranormal from stage magic), would give her control of her life, which at that point was totally out of control. Spells and rituals became a way of life for her. She noted, "I want to be very clear about this. I wasn't some kind of power-hungry control freak seeking to dominate my environment. At first I was happy, thinking that I'd encountered a positive religion with a goddess who would love me and empower me to make beneficial changes in my life. As a result, I became rather adept at casting spells."

Needless to say, Nellie Jo and I were intensely interested in this phenomenon. We had no exposure to spell-casting. But Kathi did not want us to write too much about this matter lest others become overly interested in it.

"For instance, when I was short on money I would do spell work. Within days of doing this, money would start coming in," she said.

I didn't think I would suggest this approach for fund-raising at the seminary where I worked.

Kathi cautioned that there is good reason why she doesn't want anyone to become intrigued with casting spells. The power to cast spells does not rest within the person; nor does it come from "the goddess." Plainly put, the power comes from Satan, and he does not let people borrow that power without paying a price.

Kathi was on the leading edge of Internet usage. In 1994 she started looking on the Internet for other pagans. She quickly got involved with a large pagan community on AOL. From there she started running pagan chat rooms and Wiccan discussion groups. But after a while Wicca was not enough for Kathi. "I just couldn't find spiritual fulfillment in Wicca." The next step in her pilgrimage would prove to take her deeper in the world of the occult.

> Witches do not believe that Wicca has anything to do with Satan, with the Devil. Indeed, most witches do not believe in evil, but such nonbelief does not negate the reality of evil. Witches do not practice human or animal sacrifices, though some pagan religions, such as Santeria, do practice animal sacrifices. Sometimes persons claiming to be witches get involved in more bizarre or criminal behavior, but they are often not pagans.

Wicca and the Egyptian Gods

"I wish Christians could understand how people like me are searching even when they don't admit they are," Kathi said with obvious passion. "I had this nagging hole in me that nothing could fill.

"By 1996 I had stumbled across some ancient Egyptian gods," Kathi noted. "I really felt like these gods were speaking to me. Wicca is very eclectic. That's part of what led me to explore ancient Egypt in the first place, but it turned out that these gods were very exclusive. I started spending more time with them and ultimately did not consider myself Wiccan any longer but Kemetic." (*Kemetic* refers to a particular pagan path.)

God Sends Ed

In 1997 Kathi's doctor recommended she leave the Northeast for a warmer climate due to health problems she was experiencing. She made the decision to move to North Carolina. "I was already working out of the house with this web company based in Greensboro.

My boss had no problem with my being local. The first day I arrived here it was so warm and sunny," she said with a smile.

Everyone who knows my wife and me at least casually knows that we are Florida fanatics. Our second home is in Naples, Florida. We understood Kathi's sunshine therapy well. In fact, as I listened to the recording of our interview, I was somewhat embarrassed that we had taken fifteen minutes of Kathi's time to talk about Florida. I should get stipends from the Naples Chamber of Commerce.

Fortunately, the waitress came by again. I think she was beginning to view us as family. Her interruption got us back on track to Kathi's story.

"There was this guy at work in Greensboro named Ed," Kathi continued. "He had committed to pray for me even before I moved to North Carolina. We had actually known each other online for a few years. He was in a wheelchair and would roll by the cubicle where I worked. Ed would say, 'Kathi, I'm still praying for you.'

"Well, I would fuss at him and occasionally swear. Sometimes I told him that he had no right to talk to his God on my behalf. But other times I told him that I didn't care. Or I would sarcastically smile and tell him, 'Go ahead. Talk to God.' I don't know why I was so upset since I didn't believe his God existed. That man prayed for me for years. I think he is one of the main reasons I'm a Christian today."

A New Marriage

Today Kathi is married to Ken Sharpe. They met shortly after Kathi moved to North Carolina. Ken's mother had "gotten religion" when he was a small child, and he had burned out on religion when he was a teen due to her fanaticism.

Imagine this scenario. A witch gets married to an unconverted former Southern Baptist. Some of the conversations at home must have been fascinating.

Kathi noted our curiosity about the marriage and told us one interesting conversation between the witch–Egyptian god worshiper and the unconverted ex–Southern Baptist. "I tried to cancel Easter celebrations in our home," she began. "Why not? I didn't believe Jesus ever existed, and Ken was not a Christian. What business did we have celebrating the resurrection?"

She could recall the story with a smile now. "That was the biggest fight we ever had," she said. He said, 'We can't forget Easter; it's about Jesus.' I said, 'Are you nuts?'"

Nellie Jo and I forgot to ask how the Easter controversy was resolved. But we were ready to hear more about Kathi's journey.

Deafness and an Assemblies of God Church

Kathi had been experiencing a slow but progressive hearing loss for several years. By 1999 the problem was acute. The specialists offered little hope and no definitive diagnosis. One doctor told her to start learning sign language so that she would be prepared to enter the world of total deafness. In the meantime the physicians gave her a digital hearing aid to provide her modest hearing ability.

"I began to live as a deaf person," she said. "This was not on my life's agenda. I also began to get frustrated with my gods. The gods just did not help me when times were tough. My attitude was wretched. Life was just terrible. Then matters got worse when we found out that Ken's ex-wife was taking his daughter to an Assemblies of God church. 'What else is going to go wrong?' I began asking myself."

A few days later Ken's daughter was visiting with her father and Kathi. "I was getting really upset about this Assemblies of God thing," Kathy said with animation. "I told Brandy that we needed to take custody of her from her mother. I had looked at the website for the Assemblies denomination, and I didn't like what I saw. I told Ken that those people really believed in Jesus and the Holy Spirit. I also saw a sound condemnation of many things I believed in—the occult, abortion, homosexuality, and an assortment of other sins. To me they looked like some sort of dangerous cult."

{ There is no concept of sin or the need for forgiveness in pagan traditions. There is no need for salvation. Most pagans do not believe in a literal hell or heaven. Some espouse the concept of karma and reincarnation, much like the Hindu and Buddhist beliefs.

But Ken's daughter convinced Ken and Kathi that they should go to the church before they made any judgments. Again my imagination created a humorous scene: a witch and an agnostic ex–Southern Baptist visiting a Pentecostal church.

"My first impression when I went to that church was that those people are nuts," Kathi told us in her usual frank manner. "They were really into praise and worship. My only experience in a church was two hymns, sit down, and doze, because no one listens to the preacher anyway. The members of the Assemblies of God church seemed like they would never sit down."

But Kathi began to see something else in the church. "I couldn't hear much with my hearing problem, so I began to look at the faces of the people there. I could see that they really believed this stuff. They truly believed in the Jesus they were singing about."

Kathi and Ken went back for a second visit. A missionary from Bangladesh spoke about saving Muslims. "I couldn't understand why anybody wanted to save Muslims," she remembered. "The concept was foreign to me.

"But we finally concluded that the church was not dangerous for Ken's daughter," Kathi told us. "I felt that these people were at least sincere about their beliefs. They believed the Bible, unlike the Mormons who had contradicted the Bible." Ken and Kathi did not tell anyone the reason for their visits, but a church member recognized them and began to pray for them.

When Kathi Met Jesus

In hindsight Kathi sees many events coming together that God used to bring her to salvation in Jesus Christ. Witchcraft and polytheism weren't helping her. Ed was still praying for her; someone from the church began to pray as well. Her stepdaughter influenced her to visit a church. She saw genuine Christianity in the faces of the congregants at the church. But the most dramatic event had yet to take place a few months later.

> There are many religions within the umbrella of paganism. Many are regionally influenced. Wicca and witchcraft within the United States and developed countries tend to be practiced in somewhat benign forms. Even those groups that do not hold to the Wiccan Rede tend to honor its principle of "do no harm." Other regions may practice darker forms of witchcraft. On a missions trip to Panama, Kathi discovered that the witches (brujeras and cunanderras) threaten children if parents don't pay them money. See information about the various forms of paganism at www.exwitch.org.

"In July 2000," she began, "I had a dream about Jesus. I woke up like a shot and told him to go away. But the funny thing is I didn't believe in him. So I tried to make the dream go away. I had eaten bad pizza that day, so I attributed the dream to the food and tried to laugh it off.

"Then two nights later, I had another dream about him. I knew right away who it was. At first in the dream I was incredibly afraid of him, especially after I had told him to go away. But he spoke to me in sign language. He said, 'I love you. Come follow me.'"

Allow me to pause for a moment in Kathi's story. Some of what you are about to read may stretch your imagination and beliefs. Regardless of the conclusion you derive, I must share my perspective of this portion of her testimony. Kathi has no desire to focus on the sensational aspects of her conversion. Indeed, she repeatedly steered us back to a right focus on the glory of God in her journey to Christ. But this part of her testimony is integral to understanding the dramatic way God intervened in her life.

Kathi's second dream of Jesus was on a Saturday evening. When Kathi woke up Sunday morning, she nudged Ken and told him that the family was going to church. "He thought I had lost it," she reflected.

"I was scared to death," Kathi admitted. "What if they found out I was a witch? Would they try to burn me at the stake?" With that anxiety, she entered the Assemblies of God church again. Kathi said that she went back to that church because the people really seemed to know the Jesus about whom they were singing. Besides, where else would they have gone?

"In hindsight," she commented, "it could have been a humorous scene: a deaf witch sitting in an Assemblies of God church because Jesus had appeared to her in a dream and said "follow me" in sign language, accompanied by an incredulous, agnostic, unconverted ex–Southern Baptist guy. We could've made a comic strip out of this."

Kathi read the lips of the pastor the best she could. Ken filled in some of the spots where she did not pick up the preacher's words. But really, not much of it made sense. And she was not about to ask anyone's advice. Not yet.

"I went to work Monday in a wretched state," she said slowly. "I had almost convinced myself that the dream was only a hallucination. It had no reality. But the hole in my heart had become bigger. I really needed help."

Kathi's work had not been going well. She had been given responsibility for fixing a software program that was vital to the business. Her boss, with whom she already had an adversarial relationship, was blaming Kathi for the problems of the program. Kathi sent numerous emails to people who used a similar program asking for help in getting the problem fixed.

The intersection of her spiritual and professional miseries prompted Kathi to do something she had never done previously: she prayed to God. Some would say it was more of a challenge than a prayer.

"I said to him, 'Okay, if you're really God, you can fix this software. And do it in a way that I will know that you did it.'" But no one responded to her email of desperation that day. And the prayer seemed to go unanswered.

"But when I got back from lunch on Tuesday, I had an email waiting on me," she continued. "It was from a guy whose address was at *christianity.net*. The subject said, 'Answer to Your Software Problem.' I was freaking out, because it had been several months since I'd sent out any messages to software support groups. The message simply had three lines of code. I applied it to our program, and all the problems were immediately fixed. The guy sitting next to me, another pagan, heard me exclaim in amazement and asked what was going on. I told him that God just fixed the Lyris software. He thought I had gone completely nuts.

"I sent an instant message to this guy named Rich at christianity.net and told him that he had just proven to me that God exists. He said, 'Cool.' Then I told him that I was a witch and had questions about God. I imagine you could have heard a pin drop in his office. It turns out that he had felt led by the Holy Spirit to answer that particular email at that particular time. Another incredible part of the story is that he had just completed a Christian apologetics course, so he was able to answer all my questions."

Kathi told Rich her complete story, and it did not seem to faze him. Over the next two days, she continued to ask questions, and he patiently responded. On Thursday she asked the Philippian jailer question with different words: "How does one convert to Christ?"

"Rich gave me the bare essential gospel," she said joyfully, "and I prayed the sinner's prayer from my desk at work and became a follower of Christ."

Kathi told us an amusing sidebar to this astounding story. "Before I became a Christian, I had become a bitter and sarcastic person. And I showed my greatest hatred toward my immediate boss. We couldn't stand to be in the same room with each other.

Right after I prayed the sinner's prayer, she walks into my office and I smile at her. She utters some profanity, asking me what was wrong with me. I told her I just found Jesus. She exited the room quickly."

> No one is able to estimate accurately the number of witches in America, but there is general consensus on two fronts. First, the number of witches and other pagans is growing. And second, estimates on their numbers may be forthcoming soon as more and more witches are less hesitant to make their beliefs public.

Another Miracle and Unfinished Business

"That next day," Kathi shared with us, "we left on our family vacation, camping on the beach. I found a small Assemblies of God church for us to attend. Most of the time when I lip read, I am able to follow less than half of what someone is saying. But I was able to understand every word of the preacher at this church.

"When the service was over, I spoke to him and asked him how he was able to speak so well for lip readers. He was puzzled, as he had done nothing special. I explained to him my condition of deafness, and he asked to pray for me. No one had ever done that before, but he did pray for my hearing to be restored."

Kathi and her family returned to the campground, but for some reason, Kathi started feeling sick. By the time she got to the bathhouse, she was violently ill, vomiting almost without stopping. She continued to be sick for hours, becoming more and more dehydrated.

"It was at that point that I sensed God speaking to me again," she said, choosing her words carefully. "He told me that the other gods I had been worshiping had to go. Up to that point, I had seen my conversion as a lateral move. I still had my other gods. I wasn't convinced they were evil or that paganism was wrong. But now

God said they had to go. I hesitated at first because I had become so comfortable with these other gods. They had been with me for many years."

But Kathi soon obeyed. She started calling each of the gods by the Egyptian names she knew and telling them in Jesus' name they had to go. There were many of them because the ancient Egyptians had a deity to represent every facet of life. Kathi also told anything she had worshiped as a Wiccan and anything she had remembered from the folklore of her childhood that it had to go too. "They resisted at first," she said. "But once they heard the name of Jesus, they left. As each god left, I saw them as they were, no lovely masks anymore. Instead, they had horrible, evil faces. It scared me witless. I knew then that these were no gods at all, but demons."

Immediately after they were gone, Kathi felt better. She left the bathhouse and went back to her family and began to tell her husband what had happened. When he responded, she heard every word he said—but she did not have her hearing aids in her ears. She was able to hear everything—the ocean, the birds, and her children's voices. Kathi has never stopped thanking God for what he did for her.

When she returned to the doctor who had initially treated her, he said he had never seen a condition like this reverse itself. Kathi simply said, "God did it." The doctor expressed his doubts. But Kathi knew. God did it.

Kathi had a humorous encounter with the Assemblies of God pastor when she returned to Greensboro. She had not met him; she had only visited the church. So she made an appointment to see him and introduced herself in her usual straightforward way. "I was a witch a week ago, but I'm a Christian now," she told him. "I thought I would have to pick him off the floor," she laughed as she told us the story.

Her new pastor did offer sound advice. He told her to get rid of everything connected with her witchcraft and paganism. He helped her with a plan to read the Bible. The church began to do an excellent job of discipling her.

In March of 2001 Kathi started ExWitch Ministries near Greensboro. Today she ministers to those who are experiencing the pain and hopelessness she once knew so well.

As a parting question, I asked her what advice she would give Christians who were attempting to reach the pagan community. Her counsel sounded familiar by this point in our journey. Show love to those who are hurting, even if they respond in an unloving way toward you. Have compassion as Christ modeled it in Scripture. And never forget the power of prayer.

Nellie Jo and I left Bob Evans with a renewed appreciation of both the love and power of Christ. He loved Kathi so much that he relentlessly pursued her. And he was so powerful that he defeated her gods just at the mention of his name.

Our next stop would be Columbus, Ohio, to hear the story of a former Buddhist named Helena Li. We were quiet for most of the trip to the airport. As we were getting ready to board, I said to my wife, "What an incredible story." She responded quickly, "What an incredible God."

Yeah! What an incredible God!

CHAPTER EIGHT

"MY BUDDHA STATUES STOPPED HELPING ME"

THE JOURNEY TO AMERICA AND CHRIST

September 2
Columbus, Ohio

The drive from Louisville to Columbus, Ohio, is not very excit-ing to begin with, and a heavy downpour on Interstate 71, two hundred miles from home, made the next leg of our journey even more tedious. Before our boys were grown, I had made most of my trips by myself. With more than a hundred speaking engage-ments a year, I would often find myself on rainy or snowy roads wishing the weather was better and I was back home with my wife and three sons.

But this time I was not discouraged by the redundant scenery or the bad weather. I now had the joy of Nellie Jo traveling with me. And the excitement we had discovered on each of the previ-ous seven interviews led to greater anticipation for the next con-versation. Such was my attitude as we prepared to listen to a former Buddhist.

We arrived in Columbus at 8:00 p.m. and checked into the hotel. We would be well rested for the next day's interview. The rain was still with us the following morning, but it was not as heavy as the previous evening. Our directions to the Chinese church in Columbus indicated that we were only fifteen minutes from our destination. To provide a cushion, we left thirty minutes before the scheduled appointment.

The Chinese Church and the Former Buddhist

Nellie Jo and I arrived early and went into the church and told a friendly receptionist that we were scheduled to meet Helena Li. At first my southern-midwestern twang did not communicate clearly to the Asian-American, so I said the name more slowly on the second try. She understood me and told me that I was expected.

Helena, I was told, was a layperson at the church. She had chosen the church as a good site for the interview. The church seemed to be bustling with activity on this weekday. The sign outside indicated that three services took place on Sunday morning in three different languages: Mandarin, Cantonese, and English.

> In the sixth century B.C., the son of the rulers of a small region now known as Nepal decided to explore the world beyond the palace walls. Siddhartha Gautama's journey led him to several years of deprivation, but he still had not grasped an inner peace. He decided to meditate under a bodhi tree until he discovered the answers to the questions of life. He slept in the lotus position and awoke in a state of great clarity and understanding. Siddhartha shared with others his "awakening," and they began to recognize him as one of spiritual depth and authority. They started calling him "the Buddha," which means "the Enlightened One."

I had a stereotypical image of Buddhists as being slow, methodical, and deliberate, so I anticipated an introspective and calm person when I met Helena. Was I wrong! Helena flew into the office speaking words faster than I could comprehend and led us to the church library for the interview. I had been humming to myself a slow version of "It Is Well with My Soul" in anticipation of her arrival. Jerry Lee Lewis's "Great Balls of Fire" would have been a better introduction.

Struggling in Hong Kong

Helena Li was born in Hong Kong with the given name May Hing Wong. Her family heritage was Buddhism, and she really did not consider any other religious expression during her childhood or young adulthood. I asked her to give us biographical background. This vivacious woman did not struggle for words at any point during our conversation.

"I was born into a very poor family in Hong Kong," she began with an enthusiasm that would betray the difficulties she experienced. "I was one of eight children, but two of my siblings died as children. I was number five of the remaining six. We were very poor. Our apartment was so small that we could not sit at a table together. I had to eat in the spot that was also my bed."

She continued her story. "I had a dream of having a family that could sit at one table together, even if we just had bread to eat and water to drink. But we were so poor. In Hong Kong you had to pay a monthly fee to go to school. My family never gave me the money on time, so I would be humiliated at school. Someone would say over a speaker so that the whole school could hear, 'May Hing Wong, where is your money? Why are you late with your fee?'"

Helena's mother stayed in a state of despair over the family's financial strain. She would cry regularly as she sent her daughter to school without the requisite fee. Although Buddha is not supposed to be worshiped as a god, many Buddhists seek the favor of Buddha by burning incense or paper money. Helena grew up in such an environment.

> Buddha is not a god. In fact, in Buddhism there is no concept
> of an absolute god. In many countries in Asia and Southeast
> Asia, statues of Buddha are everywhere. Buddhists bring
> offerings of incense, paper money, and flowers to the statues
> as a display of respect.

From Hong Kong to America

"My older sister made a great sacrifice for our family," Helena continued. "She married a Chinese-American citizen and moved to the United States. She immediately started doing the paperwork for us to move to America with her. It took ten years before we were allowed to immigrate. My family arrived in 1968, and because I did not have a completed application, I had to wait until 1969 to join them."

Nellie Jo wondered how difficult Helena's transition was to her new country.

Helena's eyes widened as she spoke. "Difficult! No way was it difficult. The moment I arrived in America, I began to shout, 'I love America. I love the U.S.'"

Since her family had preceded her in the United States, they had prepared her for the new country with great anticipation. "My mother told me when she arrived that she could go to work. In Hong Kong they only want the young and energetic workers. My mother got a job in a factory as a seamstress, and she was so excited. She would kiss her paycheck every time she was paid.

Helena and Buddhism

I was curious about Helena's spiritual state at the point she arrived in America. "I knew nothing but Buddhism. I only knew my Buddhas. Before I came to America, I had never heard about God or Jesus. Buddhism was a way of life for me."

Helena was like many of the "mainstream" Buddhists. While in the technical sense of the belief system there is no god to whom to direct prayers or concerns, many of the Buddhists see their Buddhas as a way to connect with something or someone else. In that regard, their Buddha statues act as a type of intermediary in a priestly function.

> Buddha gave little regard to God. While most Buddhists aren't opposed to the concept of God, they really don't consider any deity relevant. No relationship with a god is necessary, because the spiritual goal of Buddhism is self-discovery and awareness. Buddhism at its foundation is really both atheistic and nihilistic. There ultimately is no god, and nothing really exists. Such is the reason that Buddhism does not neatly fit into a general description of world religions. This belief system has no need for a deity.

When Nellie Jo asked Helena if anyone tried to share the gospel of Christ with her when she first moved to America, Helena told us one of her many humorous stories. "I was living in Chinatown in New York City," she began. "Some people came by and offered to take us to a youth camp. I was eighteen years old, and the camp looked like fun. And the price was very cheap.

"So I signed up with some of my friends. The camp was about an hour and a half outside of the city. When we first got there, the leaders told us that camp would begin with a worship service and Bible study where we would learn about Jesus. I told them they were crazy, that I was going home. They said 'fine,' but I didn't have any way to get home. I had to stay the whole time, but I didn't attend any of the functions."

The Hardworking Buddhist

We fast-forwarded Helena's story to 1977, when she met and married her husband, George. He was from a military and artistic family in Taiwan. That same year her employer, an insurance underwriter, relocated her to Columbus, Ohio. George was not employed, so he followed his new wife.

In 1981 Helena and George opened a restaurant in Columbus. The venture proved to be a great success. "We made so much money in that restaurant," Helena recalled. "I was so thankful to all of my Buddhas. I would burn incense and paper money and give them lots of food to thank them. Everything was going so smoothly in our lives."

> Buddha articulated the "Way of the Middle" as the path to enlightenment. This middle ground was a place between extreme self-denial and total self-indulgence. He stated that the Four Nobel Truths are the way to this middle:
>
> 1. Life is all about suffering.
> 2. The cause of suffering is greed.
> 3. There is a way to overcome our greed.
> 4. The path to relief of suffering is an eight-step process. The ultimate goal is to achieve nirvana, the final state of liberation from the cycle of life and suffering.

But Helena's husband did not fare well in cooler climates. He convinced Helena to sell their home and move to Naples, Florida, to open another restaurant. The good life that her Buddhas were giving her was about to come to an end.

In 1984 the Li family moved to Naples, convinced that they could make money anywhere. They had the positive experience of the Columbus restaurant, and they had their Buddhas. But the restaurant had difficulties from the onset. Helena and George were not able to replicate the success of the Columbus restaurant in Naples. Matters got worse when George became filled with frustration over their failures and took his frustration out on Helena. The trials increased as their three young daughters grew intensely homesick for their babysitter and friends in Ohio. All the money was gone. And to make the situation even more desperate, Helena discovered she was pregnant with a fourth child.

Helena began to share with us how she started having doubts about her faith. She believed that her commitment to the Buddhas was the key to her success in the past. Her loyalty and devotion had not diminished, but life was getting worse by the day. Helena did everything she could to keep the restaurant financially afloat. Despite her pregnancy, she continued to work eighteen-hour days. But the restaurant failed. Broke and disillusioned, the family decided to move to New York City.

I was listening with captivated interest to Helena's story. I couldn't wait to discover how these difficult life events would eventually lead Helena to become a Christian. But I would have to be patient. There was more to be told of her hardships.

> There are several branches of Buddhism, but they have several beliefs in common. They all hold to the belief called **samsara**, that life consists of the three components of suffering, change, and the absence of an eternal soul. They also agree on **renunciation**, the letting go of desires in life because those desires do not really exist. Buddhists commonly hold to **reincarnation**, the belief that the dead are simply reborn according to their karma. **Nirvana** is the breaking of the cycle of death and reincarnation. Most Buddhists hold to this belief, but its precise meaning is elusive.

Back to Ohio and More Problems

"We decided to move back to Ohio when a former employee asked me to help him open a restaurant," Helena continued, "but our family was ashamed to be back in Columbus. When we lived there the first time, we were great success stories. We had a nice house, nice car, and a country club membership. Now we were coming back broke, in debt, with no nice house to live in. People starting asking me what had happened to us. I was so ashamed."

Then the struggling wife and mother received some more difficult news. She was pregnant with her fifth daughter. "I should not have been medically able to have this child," she recalled. "I was shocked when I found this out."

Helena seemed as if she needed a break from the recollection of these difficult years. Intuitively, Nellie Jo asked her if she had pictures of her daughters. In a flash of motherly pride, she retrieved a photograph of all of her daughters together. Nellie Jo and I looked at and admired the beautiful girls.

But Nellie Jo took a second look. "Wait a minute," my wife requested. She took the photo in her hand. "One, two, three, four, five . . . six. Helena, there are six girls in the picture."

Helena smiled. "I guess you will have to hear the rest of the story.

"Everything was going wrong. I stopped working with the man opening a restaurant, and I took two jobs as a waitress. George did not work, but I worked two full-time shifts. A year later I was pregnant. And to make matters worse, George had to return to Taiwan with medical problems. The owner of the restaurant had left me with the responsibility of waiting on tables and managing the place. I was working sixteen-hour days seven days a week."

The frustration grew in Helena's life. "I started talking to my Buddha: 'Give me a sign. Help me get through these awful times.'"

The fifth daughter was born in 1989. Helena suffered nerve damage in her hip during the delivery. Life was getting so difficult for her that she made a trip to a Buddhist fortune-teller in Chicago to see if her life would ever get better. After getting her future viewed, Helena was told to leave money for the fortune-teller's Buddha. "I knew who would get that money," she mused.

Helena's fortunes continued to deteriorate. "I found out that I was pregnant again, and again it should not have been medically possible." Despite doctor's orders otherwise, she continued to work sixteen- and eighteen-hour days. She worked until the day the next baby came. "She weighed almost ten pounds and was twenty-one and a half inches long. I had a big baby inside me," she said with her usual energetic voice. Helena returned to work two weeks later, and she had to depend on friends to help care for her girls.

> Although Buddhism has few doctrinal beliefs, there are three cardinal principles upon which the religion has its foundation. The principles are known as the *tiratna*, or three jewels, because they are viewed as the most valuable beliefs. The first jewel is the appreciation of Buddha who found the path of enlightenment. The second jewel is **dharma**, the teaching of the Buddhist true way. The third jewel is **sangha**, the community of monks, nuns, and others who teach and practice the dharma.

"My life was a story of ups and downs," she told us. "I wish I had known Jesus. He might not have taken me away from these problems, but he would have given me the strength to endure the trials." Helena jumped up from the interview to retrieve her Chinese-American Bible. "This verse would have given me what I needed," she said. She then read to us Job 1:21: "Naked came I from my mother's womb, and naked I shall return. The LORD gave and the LORD has taken away. Blessed be the name of the LORD."

A Change in Attitude toward Christ

Helena ultimately gave up her restaurant jobs for an opportunity to be an interpreter for five hospitals in the Columbus area. She stayed on call for physicians or other hospital personnel who needed to communicate with someone who spoke Mandarin or Cantonese. Helena was fluent in both of those languages as well as English.

Although her work life improved, life at home was still difficult. Her husband, George, continued to refuse to work. "He stayed on the sofa watching television most of the day," she recalled. They divorced in 1998.

"I had a lot of Christian customers when I worked in the restaurants. Some of those customers told me that they were praying for me," she reflected. "I told them that my Buddha gave me strength, but they said they would pray for me anyway. I learned later that many of them were praying for me to become a Christian."

Helena was telling us that her attitude toward Christians and Christ was changing. Indeed, she had come a long way from the youth camp in New York when she was eighteen. Love and concern expressed toward Helena were most likely what opened her heart to be more receptive to an invitation to church three years later. And the events of those next three years caused her to desire something greater in her life.

"I continued to work, work, work," Helena said with recollections of deep frustration. "I was a single mother. I had six daughters to care for. I had to provide for them financially. I never got to rest. I felt I had the weight of the world on my shoulders. I was so tired." She was certainly ready for help and strength.

> One of the two major traditions of Buddhism, followed by those in Tibet and in Northern Asia, including China and Japan, is called **Mahayana**. One of the tenets of Mahayana is the recognition of the role of the **bodhisattva**. The term refers to someone who is destined for enlightenment as Buddha was. The best known bodhisattva is Avalokiteshvara, whom Tibetan Buddhists believe is incarnated in the Dalai Lama. Tibetan Buddhists also emphasize the use of the mantra while meditating. The single syllables **Aum** or **om** are common mantras.

Helena Meets Christ

By 2001 Helena was exhausted and seemingly out of options to turn her life around. A coworker then asked her if she would attend the Chinese church where an evangelist was speaking. "I looked at her and said, 'Are you kidding? Not me,'" she recalled.

But Helena's resistance was nothing like it had been when she first came to America more than thirty years earlier. She put her coworker to the test. "I told her that if she bought me breakfast before church, I would go. She said 'Okay.'"

I interrupted the story Helena was telling. "Let me see if I got this right," I said to her. "This coworker just invites you, a lifelong Buddhist, to go to church, and you agree. Is that right?"

She responded simply, "Yes."

Not satisfied, I followed with another question.

"Had anyone ever invited you to church before?" I asked.

"No," she said.

"So you went to church the first time you were ever invited?" I asked again.

"That's right," she responded quickly.

I was amazed. Yet it was the story I had heard time and time again. The lost and unchurched are, as a group, highly receptive to overtures from Christians. They are likely to go to church with us if they are invited, especially if we walk into the church building with them. This lifelong Buddhist did so. How much more likely are other unchurched people to respond to our invitations?

Probably unclear as to my line of questioning, Helena resumed her conversation. "This evangelist presented the gospel so clearly. I didn't doubt for a moment the message I was hearing. I just started crying. I raised my hand when the evangelist asked if anyone wanted to accept Christ.

"When I was leaving the church, another coworker asked me to come to a class for new believers. During that class I realized what had happened to me. I had run away from God for forty-nine years. I started crying and shaking all over. The greatest relief came to me. My sins had been forgiven, and God would take the burdens of my life for me."

Helena paused for a moment and then added, "That is something Buddha never did for me. All of my life I had this burden of guilt on me. Now it was gone."

Helena jumped again to get her Chinese-American Bible. This woman could run circles around me! She was so full of energy. "Look," she said. "Look at this verse. Nellie Jo, you read it."

My wife complied. "Come to me, all you who are weary and burdened, and I will give you rest," she read from Matthew 11:28.

"That is something my Buddha could never do," Helena said with a smile.

The New Christian and a New Ministry

"I had the perfect job to share Christ," she continued. "I interpreted for hospital patients who spoke Mandarin and Cantonese. But the job did not let me talk about Jesus. What I did, though, was ask a patient if he would like for someone from the Chinese community to visit him. If he said yes, I would call the church, and someone would come or call and share the gospel with him."

> The second main branch of Buddhism is called **Theravada**, which means "doctrine of the elders." These Buddhists focus on service and compassion to others. The followers of Theravada are found in the countries of Southeast Asia and in Sri Lanka. They are closely tied together through the work of monks and laypersons.

Helena's ministry is unlike any job she previously held. From the moment she came to America, she had pursued the capitalist dream of making money. But her new work includes much more. She still has to focus on the financial needs of her family ("I have to get the rest of the girls through college"), but her work is also a ministry.

"God is blessing me so much," she said. "I am able to make money and to be a witness for Christ. I knew that people noticed the change in my life when they stopped me in the hallways of the hospitals. They asked me why I had such a big smile on my face. I have been able to cheer up sick patients just with this big smile that Jesus has given me."

Tying Up Loose Ends

A visiting preacher came from Hong Kong to speak at Helena's church. "He said some things that made me feel uncomfortable," she told us. "I still had many Buddhas in my house and sensed that it was wrong to have them there."

Although a crowd was waiting to speak with the preacher, Helena patiently waited her turn. She told him that she had become a Christian but that she still had many Buddha statues in her home. The preacher responded that she must destroy all of them as soon as possible.

"I told him that I only used them as decorations. They were beautiful, and many of them were expensive. One of them cost three thousand dollars several years ago. But he told me that I had to remove all connections to my Buddhist life. He said, 'If you trust Jesus, make your house clean.'"

The preacher and Helena actually scheduled a service at her home to destroy the statues. Several couples from the church attended. They sang hymns, read Scripture, prayed, and then put all the statues into several large trash bags. Several of the friends and Helena took hammers and battered the statues in the bags to pieces.

"I felt like my house was clean, like I had become clean," she said with a smile. But Helena still had one major piece of unfinished business to handle. "George had been a terrible husband, but I knew I had to forgive him. You know, when I started praying to God to give me the strength to forgive him, it was not nearly as hard as I thought it would be. Jesus forgave me, and I forgave George. Love is the connection from God."

Nellie Jo, always interested in the health of the family, asked, "What do you see for you and George in the future?" Helena responded softly, "My family priority right now is to get the youngest four girls through college. I don't really have time to think about my own personal life."

She paused a moment and resumed. "But if he gets help for his anger, and if he becomes a Christian, I might remarry him. We will just have to see. I am taking it one day at a time. But now I have Jesus with me."

> Because Buddhists are not organized into churches or similar groups, exact counts are difficult. There are probably more than 300 million Buddhists worldwide and 500,000 in the United States. It is the dominant religion in China, Japan, Korea, and the countries of Southeast Asia. Buddhism is also the largest religion in Hawaii.

Christians Reaching Buddhists

By this point in our conversations for the *Journey*, I had developed my own tradition for closing the interviews. If the interviewees had not already told us explicitly, I asked them how Christians could best reach those of other religions. The vivacious former Buddhist was happy to offer her insights.

"A Christian needs to tell Buddhists that they can talk directly to Jesus, that they can have a personal relationship with him," she shared without hesitation. "Buddhists have no concept of a personal God, someone that they can talk to. I tell Buddhists that I can talk to my God anytime and any day. I do not have to burn incense and paper money, and give food and talk to my statue as a middleman."

> Zen Buddhism, though not the largest expression of Buddhism in the United States, gets much publicity. This form of Buddhism focuses on learning one's true self from meditation. The teachings and doctrines of others should be ignored, and you should have the personal experience of discovery for yourself.

Helena gave us another illustrative insight. "If you talk to a Buddhist, compare our heavenly Father to a good earthly father," she said. "Ask them if the children of loving parents have to buy the parents things in order to talk to them. That's what we do with our Buddhas. We buy incense and burn paper money. But a true and loving Father hears his children unconditionally."

Finally, the pervasive theme of love came up. Helena reminded us that the love of praying Christians, the love of a Christian co-worker, and the love of church members were powerfully influential in her conversion.

"My life was in such a mess," Helena recalled. "I had a terrible marriage. Our family was in awful financial shape. I was working myself to the point of exhaustion. I cried all the time. I just felt like I was carrying all the burdens of the world on my shoulders.

"Now I have a good job. All of my girls are Christians. But, most of all, I have Jesus. Even when life is not perfect, he is my strength. He is my hope. What more could I ever ask for?"

The rain had stopped as Nellie Jo and I left the Chinese church in Columbus. I wouldn't attempt to make too much of the weather change except to offer a metaphor. Like Helena's life, the clouds and storms had given way to warmth and light. And her life had been radically changed by a personal God who loves his children unconditionally.

"Where to next?" Nellie Jo asked with anticipation. I told her that I had some six weeks of speaking engagements before the next *Unexpected Journey* interview. Her face registered clear disappointment. I hoped I was not getting the wrong message. Was my wife telling me that she would rather hear the testimony of a stranger than her own husband's messages and speeches? Surely not.

The next conversation would take place with a former Unitarian. She had graciously offered to fly to Louisville to save us another long trip. The journey continues.

CHAPTER NINE

"IT SEEMED TO BE SUCH A HUMBLE APPROACH TO GOD"

THE JOURNEY FROM UNITARIANISM TO CHRIST AND THE TRINITY

October 15
Louisville, Kentucky

I was weary. I worry sometimes that I complain about my travels, that I take my speaking and consulting opportunities for granted. Indeed, I never would have dreamed several years ago that I would be living the incredible life that God has given me. It is such an undeserved gift from my Lord. I cannot take it for granted.

But I was still weary.

In less than six weeks since our last interview, Nellie Jo and I had traveled to fourteen states, sixteen cities, and Canada. I was ready for some time at home. My unspoken prayer was answered.

Dr. Karan Townsend, a former Unitarian from Washington, D.C., graciously offered to fly to Louisville for her interview. While I gladly would have flown to D.C. to hear her amazing story, I was very grateful for her offer, which I accepted gladly.

The added bonus of conducting an interview in Louisville was having my son, Jess, and his girlfriend, Rachel McNeil, attend the interview with Nellie Jo and me. Jess was home from college, a rare event for my youngest son. He is preparing for the ministry, so this interview was a great opportunity for him.

A Very Smart Woman Named Karan

My first one-word impression of Karan Townsend was "energetic." My second was "smart." By the time our interview concluded, I felt certain that my initial impressions were accurate if not understated.

Karan was an unlikely Unitarian. Born in the Bible Belt of central Texas in Lockhart, just south of Austin, she thought that everyone was a Christian. "Before going to college, I never considered that there were other 'respectable' religious options," Karan mused.

> *Unitarianism is the belief that God exists as one person, not three. It therefore denies the doctrine of the Trinity as well as the divinity of Jesus Christ. Although some Unitarians may call themselves "Christian," they do not hold to the biblical view that Jesus is the Son of God who offers the only way of salvation.*

Karan was active in church all of her youth. "Everyone thought I was a true Christian," she said, "and I guess I did too." Karan accepted biblical doctrinal truths such as the virgin birth and the resurrection of the dead with confidence that she would understand them better when she got older. But she had no conviction of her need for a Savior. Rather than better understand these doctrines, Karan rejected all she had been taught about Christ soon after she graduated from high school.

To College and Unitarianism

Karan Townsend spent a major segment of her life (1967 to 1981) on the campus of the University of Houston. She completed her bachelor's, master's, and doctoral degrees at Houston and took a position in the College of Education there. The first shaping event at college took place after she had been on campus for only a month.

"Like many state universities," Karan began, "the University of Houston is very secular. There may have been some Christian groups on the campus, but I didn't know anything about them."

Immersed in the philosophy and psychology of secular humanism, Karan began meeting some fellow intellectuals on campus, and then she started attending a church where many of them also attended. "Within only a few months, I rejected the inspiration and inerrancy of the Bible, the miracles, and the deity of Christ. I continued to believe in the existence of God though. I was never agnostic; I was never polytheistic," she reflected.

At this point in the interview, I interrupted with apologies. I was not ready to continue our conversation without some clarification.

"Let me see if I understand you correctly," I said. "In just a few months' time, you had rejected historical Christianity and embraced the beliefs of Unitarianism." Karan affirmed my statement. "What or who was so influential that caused this dramatic change?" I asked.

Whenever Karan spoke she had an obvious energy and enthusiasm. I could see that she would never accept something half-heartedly. She was either in all the way or not at all.

"When I met these Unitarians and attended their church, everything they said just seemed to make sense and seemed to be reinforced in general by the campus culture," she told us. "I was captivated by their inclusivity and open-mindedness as well as their emphasis on pluralism and the integrity of one's own mind and conscience. Unitarianism just seemed to be such a humble approach to God. You never claimed you really knew who God is, and you accepted with serious interest and respect the beliefs of others."

The church Karan was attending was a Unitarian Universalist church. This denomination was the result of a merger of two groups that had similar but not identical beliefs. "It is really a very intellectual approach to religion," she explained. "All Unitarians are on their own spiritual quest and no one is wrong."

> Unitarian Universalist became a denomination in 1961 when the American Unitarian Association merged with the Universalist Church of America. Membership is approximately 200,000 today.

Nellie Jo was curious about the reaction of Karan's family to her new religious path. "They never really knew what was going on," she responded. "The Unitarian church I attended had enough of the familiar liturgy and the religious words and music to satisfy my parents. They never commented about my church when they would visit with me."

Karan also explained that Unitarian churches are not identical in their perspectives. "Members of the church I attended were basically respectable, conservative, and moral citizens. That seemed to pacify my parents."

Becoming an Active Unitarian

The words *passive* and *lackluster* are not in Dr. Karan Townsend's vocabulary. Once she began to embrace the basic tenets of Unitarianism, she became an enthusiastic proponent of her newfound religion. "It just seemed so profound and so helpful," she reflected. "I thought this very intellectual approach to searching for God just made good sense."

Karan began to get involved with the Unitarian Universalist church with passion. She listened with interest as one week she heard a message on Native American religions, the next week a message about reconciliation among humans, and the next week a story from the Bible from a person who did not hold to the authority of the Bible.

> The Universalist part of the merger of the two denominations in 1961 represented those who believed that because all human beings are loved by God, everyone will go to heaven, though the adherents held many differing definitions of heaven.

Almost any religious teaching was on the table in Karan's church. "About the only doctrine that we all held was that there is one God," she said. "But it seemed that the more I spoke with people about their understanding of God, the more I realized that no one really had the same idea. God was just whomever or whatever you perceived him to be. Since I did not believe the Bible was inspired and inerrant, I was totally satisfied with my theology and my relationship with God."

Karan loved this openness to faith and God. She loved the willingness to embrace different parts of many different religions and philosophies. At one point she taught a Sunday school class on the Bible. "We felt like we needed to know something about all faiths, especially Christianity," she said with enthusiasm. "So I led a class to learn the basics about all the books of the Bible."

Nellie Jo asked a question as Karan paused. "Did you believe any parts of the Bible?"

Karan responded quickly, "Oh, absolutely. The Great Commandment was a major part of my worldview. Our church was very focused on causes and community needs. We often used texts from the Bible to support our deeds."

The pattern that Karan began to follow is congruent with most Unitarian teachings. There is no authority outside of human reasoning. The Bible can thus be accepted or rejected in part or in whole by the reader.

> In Unitarianism human reasoning and experience are the final
> authorities in determining spiritual truths. In the end, reli-
> gious authority cannot be found in a book or in a person.
> Instead, ultimate authority comes from within the human and
> his or her own search for truth.

The Adult Unitarian and Perspectives on Christianity

Karan refers to her early adult years as a Unitarian as "the good
life." She is not suggesting that she would trade her current status
as a follower of Christ to revert to her old beliefs; she is referring
to the privileges of life that were hers as a young adult.

She continued to be active in her Unitarian congregation. She
met and eventually married an attorney of like beliefs. In a few
years, she would give birth to two sons and a daughter.

"It really was the good life from many perspectives," she
recalled. "The college was a great place to be for intellectual and
professional challenges and rewards. I married a brilliant attorney
who was a devoted father to our three children. He provided well
for us, settling us comfortably in a lovely home in an ideal neighborhood."

The interaction of her children with other children in the
schools brought Karan back into contact with Christians and
Christian congregations. On occasion she would find herself in
these churches for events for her children. The experiences were
not good.

"I really felt uncomfortable in these churches," Karan told us.
"Even from my Unitarian perspective, most of the churches I saw
were unhealthy. I saw the people in the churches as nonintellec-
tual, materialistic, hypocritical, and superficial: pretty on the outside but hollow on the inside. I wondered how they could sing the
songs they sang, how they could believe the things they said.

"I would love to go back and visit these churches now, three
decades later. My first focus would be on the pastor. I couldn't stay

in a church led by a pastor whose preaching and teaching failed to help me understand the Bible more than I understood it when I finished confirmation classes at age fourteen."

Nellie Jo was curious about Karan's perspective of her own spiritual path. "How did you see yourself?" my wife asked.

"I was searching for God," Karan responded. "I believed that no one could really know God, so my path was the most honest and exciting."

"Did you pray to God?" Nellie Jo inquired.

"Oh, I prayed to God consistently," Karan told her. "I just was not certain to whom I was praying. I was perfectly happy to be open and challenged in this way."

> Most Unitarians believe that searching for God and struggling to know God are signs of intellectual honesty. Unitarians typically keep an open mind to all religions and all religious questions. The belief system is anticreedal, because a creed is a set of agreed-upon and known beliefs. The basis of agreement among Trinitarians is a set of beliefs or a creed. The basis of agreement among Unitarians is not having a creed.

A Daughter Searches and a Cousin Prays

Karan left Houston for a research, development, and teaching job that took her and her daughter to Salzburg, Austria, for several years and then to locations in Eastern Europe. "My daughter was on her own spiritual journey," Karan remembered with a smile. "I encouraged her in her quest. That was the Unitarian way, always searching.

"Unitarianism says that we must always be on a journey, always searching, because we can never really know God," Karan said. "But Christianity claims to have and to know truth. These two positions are incongruent."

The "problem" was that Karan's daughter was being drawn to the teachings of Christ and the beliefs of Christianity. "I was going back and forth between Texas, Virginia, and Eastern Europe for my research project," Karan continued. "My daughter was visiting monasteries in Europe in her search, but her search actually came to an end in Virginia."

I sensed we were getting close to Karan's story about her own conversion. I was captivated. I looked around my office and saw that Nellie Jo, Jess, and Rachel all were watching Karan with anticipation. We waited as Karan explained what transpired in Virginia.

> As a denomination, Unitarian Universalists affirm several principles, though they would not likely call these tenets "truths": the inherent worth and dignity of every person, justice and compassion in human relationships, complete acceptance of one another, free and responsible search for truth, use of the democratic process and conscience in congregational life, and the goal of a peaceful world community.

"When we returned to the United States, my daughter stayed with my cousin and her family so that she could attend the nearby high school while I traveled between Europe and the United States," Karan told us. "My cousin was praying for both of us and gently pointing us to sources that defended the Christian faith."

But it was Karan's daughter who first became a Christian.

"My daughter had been searching for some time," Karan reminded us. "And while she was staying with my cousin, they began attending church together. The church my cousin belonged to was an evangelical, charismatic Episcopal congregation."

Although all *The Unexpected Journey* stories are profound, they all seem to have a bit of humor as well. I didn't interrupt Karan's story, but I found myself smiling at the scenario she described: a Unitarian sitting in an evangelical, charismatic Episcopal church. God does have a sense of humor.

We did not ask for many of the details of her daughter's pilgrimage, but we did hear the most important part. "She became a

Christian in the fall of 1995," Karan told us. That event and the gentle persistence of Karan's cousin would soon lead her down that same path.

A Unitarian Meets Christ

"During my trips to Virginia, I always offered to help my busy cousin with her chores and errands" Karan resumed, "but she said no. She said that she wanted me to sit back and read some books."

The first book Karan read was *Surprised by Joy* by C. S. Lewis. She then followed that book with three more by Lewis: *The Screwtape Letters*, *Mere Christianity*, and finally, *The Great Divorce*.

"I began to see myself," Karan said, now speaking at a much more deliberate pace. "I could see where Satan had taken me over the years when I read *The Screwtape Letters*. Then *Mere Christianity* helped me to see clearly the basics of Christianity.

"I guess the single turning point was Lewis's convincing argument that I could not accept Christ as a great prophet or a great man. Christ himself claimed to be God. So he was either a liar, lunatic, or, as he claimed, the Son of God.

"Everything was just so convincing," Karan recalled. "It was like coming home. In January 1996 I said yes to Christ."

> Historically both Unitarians and Universalists have held that Jesus was a God-filled human being, but that he was not a supernatural being and certainly not deity. Today the views of Christ held by Unitarians are very diverse.

For Karan that moment in January 1996 was the most vivid on her spiritual quest. That was the moment she made a volitional decision to become a follower of Christ. But we must not forget the events that preceded this decision.

God used Karan's good relationship with her cousin to bring about this conversion. "My cousin kept after me," Karan recalled. "Her long-term persistence had an impact on me. First, she not

888888888888

only modeled but also discussed with me her Christian lifestyle, including her struggles. I thought she was so radical if not downright weird in her beliefs. She talked about God all the time. She prayed all the time. She went to church all the time. She was living the life of a true Christian." Karan emphasized, "I was attracted to that even though I was repelled at the same time. There was just something different about her.

"Second, she led my daughter to Christ. I raised all my kids to be good Unitarians," Karan reiterated. "My daughter was always encouraged to be open in all beliefs as she searched. So when she got around some healthy Christians, she converted. I was impressed and curious about the conversion of my brilliant and spirited daughter."

Karan also noted the importance of her cousin's prayer for her salvation: "My salvation was of the Holy Spirit, but my cousin was praying that the Holy Spirit would convict me. She also encouraged me to attend a healthy church where I was exposed to a strong community of Christians."

I looked over at Jess and noticed that he seemed uncertain about something. I was about to encourage him to interject in the conversation, but he didn't wait on me. "The whole point of Unitarianism, it seems, is to search for truth," my son stated. "What happens when you find truth?"

That was a good question. I'm glad he got his brains from his mother.

Karan smiled. "I guess you can't admit you've found it, because you would no longer be a Unitarian. According to Unitarians you can't really know truth or God during this life."

Karan paused for a moment and then recalled a specific presentation at the D.C. church she now attends. "I used to think that I was so humble because I said I could not know God," she recalled. "But now I realize how arrogant I was because I refused to see God as he has revealed himself to us. Don Carson spoke at our church on postmodernity and said, 'Just because we can't know all truth doesn't mean that we can't accept God's revelation in Scripture as absolute truth.' Unitarians refuse to believe that absolute truth can be known."

> *Unitarianism draws from many world religions. Historically, the single premise that has held Unitarians together is the belief in a god who is one person. But today some Unitarian Universalist congregations offer affiliation to those who are unwilling to affirm the existence of any deity. Such individuals are on their own pursuit of truth.*

Reaching Unitarians Today

Our primary quest in *The Unexpected Journey* is to hear the stories of those who have become Christians from other beliefs. As you have traveled these paths with us, you have heard the inspiring stories of men and women who have made a major and unexpected turn in their lives. None of our interviewees would have expected it, but all have become followers of Christ.

While listening to the stories of their conversions has been our primary goal, we also want to hear how we can best reach people in similar places today. And who better to tell us than someone who has become a Christian from one of these other beliefs? Therefore we asked Karan how we can best reach Unitarians today. She cited two factors.

"First, remember that Unitarianism is a very diverse religion," Karan reminded us. "You can meet many different Unitarians in different parts of the country and the world. Don't assume that one Unitarian's beliefs are identical to another.

> *Universalists organized as a denomination in 1793. Unitarians became a denomination in 1825. The merged denomination of 1961 has more of the characteristics of the Unitarian denomination than the older Universalist denomination.*

"Understand that most people who have Unitarian beliefs are not members of Unitarian Universalist churches. Many of the spiritual people I meet are Unitarians even if they don't call themselves that. Some would best be called New Age; others belong to some Eastern religions. But all are open and are on a spiritual quest as I was."

This spiritual quest is a crucial component for reaching Unitarians.

"This gives you an excellent opportunity to encourage them to look at the facts of Christianity," Karan said. "My cousin knew that I was searching. That gave her the insight to ask me to read the C. S. Lewis books. She knew that a truly open-minded person will read and investigate other religious claims."

At this point Karan brought up the second factor. She recalled her negative experiences with Christian congregations and commented that she had met others who had experiences similar to hers. "So I have to tell these people that they can't judge Christianity by the churches they have experienced in the past. Sometimes people have to get over bad Christians and churches before they can see Christ.

"I think if I had seen healthy churches and been close to thoughtful 'real' Christians, I would have been attracted to the faith much earlier."

Nellie Jo interjected, "You responded to someone you knew, someone who was willing to invest time with you and show love toward you."

Karan nodded affirmatively.

"She also provided resources for you. The C. S. Lewis books had a major impact on you," Nellie Jo noted.

Again, Karan agreed.

I said nothing, but I was thinking much along the same lines as Karan. If most non-Christians could see real Christianity in us, many more people would be attracted to the faith.

Karan is now in a strong evangelical church in Washington, D.C. Her enthusiasm for her relatively new faith is far greater than she ever had for Unitarianism. She expressed her gratitude toward God many times for both saving her and allowing her to find a church where she can grow as a disciple of Christ. Not surprisingly, the church was recommended to her by her cousin. The power of a persistent witness was used by God once again to bring someone to his Son, Jesus Christ.

The power of Christ continues to amaze me. This energetic Unitarian rejected her former beliefs and embraced Christianity with a contagious enthusiasm. Repeatedly in our conversation, she would tell us that only God could do what he did in her life. But there is more to this story.

Karen and her husband had divorced sometime earlier. Eventually her two sons became followers of Christ. They thought their mother "had gone crazy" when she accepted Christ. But they soon saw the Savior as the way of their salvation.

One of the reasons Karan was happy to interview with us in Louisville is that she wanted to see the Southern Baptist Theological Seminary campus. Her son has been called to the gospel ministry, and he will soon continue his training at the seminary where I work.

Who would have imagined it? An ardent proponent of the Unitarian faith is now a follower of Christ. And her three children, all raised as Unitarians, are Christians as well. One of those children is now preparing for the gospel ministry. And from a human perspective, it all began with one woman who cared enough for the salvation of her cousin that she prayed for her, showed Christian love toward her, and provided resources that would introduce her to the God of all salvation.

I turned off the recording equipment. The time had passed so quickly that Nellie Jo, Jess, Rachel, and I had hardly moved during the entire conversation. We all began to stand and stretch at the same time.

Nine interviews had taken place. Nellie Jo and I agreed that two powerful truths had emerged. First, the power of Christian love was a story line in most of our interviews. In one way or another, the theme of love was sounded with clarity.

Second, my wife and I had become convicted that we should never assume that any person is too difficult to reach. We had interviewed nine people thus far, people whom many Christians would have perceived as impossible to reach. We were discovering that spiritual hunger for truth was pervasive, even in the lives of people who seemed, on the surface, to have no interest in spiritual matters.

As Karan and my family said our farewells, we were again filled with gratitude to speak with and listen to people who had extraordinary stories of an awesome God who has done an amazing work in their lives. Karan's story was no exception.

I walked out of my office and asked my secretary, Kathy Fredrick, for the date of my next interview. She told me that it was three weeks away. I was disappointed that so much time would elapse before the next leg of *The Unexpected Journey* continued.

But the wait would be worthwhile. We would be traveling to Arlington, Virginia, not too far from Karan's home, to hear the story of someone who had spent much of her life in astrology and New Age beliefs. By now you, the reader, have come to expect the unexpected. Marsha Montenegro's story is truly an account of an unexpected journey. I'm glad you don't have to wait three weeks to hear it.

CHAPTER TEN

"ASTROLOGY WAS MY IDENTITY"

THE UNEXPECTED JOURNEY FROM NEW AGE TO CHRIST

November 4
Arlington, Virginia

On the one hand, I am prone to whine about my travel schedule. On the other hand, I get antsy when I am at home for a lengthy time. I understand that "lengthy" is a relative term. For me it means just a little over a week. I was glad to be traveling again.

Our next stop on *The Unexpected Journey* was the beautiful state of Virginia. We flew to Virginia Beach and then drove to Arlington the next day.

The first day in Virginia was a beautiful fall day. The leaves were changing colors nearly at peak viewing. We were disappointed that our drive from Virginia Beach to Arlington on the second day was a trip with perpetual torrential downpours. Because of the rain, our one-hour cushion for our scheduled appointment was completely gone. Fortunately, we arrived at the designated location only five minutes late.

The interview was scheduled to take place in a large church in Arlington. I tried three different doors in the downpour; each was locked. On the fourth door was a note stating that the thunderstorms had knocked out all the power in the church, so they were closed for the day.

I was both frustrated and confused. Would the entire flight and drive be for naught? As I was preparing to leave, a woman ran toward her car from the church building. She, like me, had not expected to see the church doors closed. As she was about to get into her car, she looked at us, and we rolled down the window. "You wouldn't be Dr. and Mrs. Rainer?" she asked. We found her. Or she found us. The show could go on.

Out of the Rain and into the French Restaurant

The first order of business was to find a place to have the interview. Our new acquaintance suggested we follow her to a quiet restaurant. I was happy to do so. I sure didn't know where to go.

About one mile from the church was a neat area of Arlington with many quaint shops and restaurants. Unfortunately, any street shopping would result in an unwanted rain bath. We ran into the restaurant.

As I got my bearings, I realized that I was in a French restaurant. I have nothing against French restaurants, but as I said earlier, meat, potatoes, and diet soda are my three main food groups. My wife saw the look of panic on my face and quietly assured me that she would find something edible for me. The nearly indistinguishable smile on her face told me that she had found a perverse pleasure in seeing me in a restaurant that did not have "Texas" or "steakhouse" in the name.

Marcia Montenegro is one of those persons you feel as if you have known a long time after just a few minutes. She has an effervescent personality that just makes you feel comfortable. She assured us that the heavy traffic in the restaurant would soon abate and the place would be quieter.

We placed our orders. I said a verbal prayer for our conversation and our food. Then I said a silent prayer that I could handle the food my wife suggested. The recording equipment was turned on. The next few hours would truly be captivating. I began with a simple request that Marcia tell us something about her background in the New Age Movement.

> The New Age, sometimes called the New Age Movement, is not as easy to define as more organized religions. It has no holy book, no central headquarters, no formal membership, no creed, and no clergy. It is a system of fluid beliefs that draws from Eastern religions, Gnosticism, and the occult, and it also has a wide variety of practices. New Agers typically do not believe in a personal god, but in a god who is an energy source, a god that can be found within us.

Meet Marcia the Former New Ager

"My father served in the foreign service for the State Department," Marcia began. "So my early years were spent in several places around the world. His father was a Chilean journalist who had seen many religious abuses. So my father grew up in a home with a father who was a devout atheist and negative toward religions."

Nellie Jo asked if Marcia's father had any religious inclinations when she was young.

"Not really," she responded. "I would describe him as an intellectual agnostic. My mother, on the other hand, grew up Southern Baptist. But I saw no Christian fruit in her life. I never saw her read the Bible or pray. I would describe her as a nominal Christian—in name only."

Although Marcia's mother showed little evidence of true Christianity in her life, she still insisted that her children attend church. "I went to church and to Sunday school regularly beginning in my early teens," Marcia continued. "I studied my Sunday school lessons; I attended Sunday evening services. I had it in my head that I had to be good to get into heaven. I took church very seriously, but the gospel message just went right over me."

Nellie Jo asked if her agnostic father had any opposition to Marcia attending church. "No," she said quickly. "He was pretty open to us doing anything religiously as long as it didn't involve the supernatural." Marcia was about to disappoint her father.

Rejecting Christianity and Embracing New Age

"By the time I was in high school, I started making friends with girls of other religions," she told us. "Among my closest friends were a Mormon, a Baha'i, a freethinker, and a strong pacifist Quaker. I started wondering why I had to be stuck with Christianity. Why couldn't I investigate other religions?"

By her senior year of high school, Marcia had rejected Christianity completely. "I began by doubting the Bible and the doctrine of hell in particular," she recalled. "And when I got to college, I began exploring Eastern religions and paranormal activities. I had become a true New Ager in the sense that I jumped from one thing to another."

> Different New Agers will tell you of different influences on their beliefs. The most common are astrology, channeling, Hinduism, Gnosticism, Taoism, Theosophy, Wicca, and other neo-pagan traditions.

Of all the experiences that Marcia had, the one that captivated her interest the most was astrology. That interest would become a career when she graduated from college and moved to Atlanta.

Nellie Jo asked Marcia what she was seeking during this time of jumping from one belief to another.

"I guess I was seeking something spiritual and supernatural," she responded. "I was particularly interested in paranormal activity."

We were briefly interrupted to eat the food that had just arrived. Nellie Jo commented that her chicken salad sandwich was great. I made several attempts to recognize the culinary offering placed before me. I got a second cappuccino with extra whipped cream in the event I could not consume my solid food.

Marcia's spiritual pilgrimage took her to a class on inner life consciousness. She was more fully introduced to Eastern meditation, dream analysis, psychic healing, remote healing, and chanting. She was also led every night in guided visualization. On the final evening of the class, Marcia learned that she would meet her spiritual master. "I did meet him," she said, "and he stayed with me for years. The first time I saw him in my visions, he looked very kind and benevolent. I felt very connected to him. I constantly felt his presence. Only in hindsight do I realize that I was dealing with a dangerous demonic presence."

Marcia's next stop was a time of experimentation in Tibetan Buddhism. "I had become a typical New Ager, absorbing one teaching and going on to another. If someone asked me what my religion was, I would tell them that I was into Tibetan Buddhism, but I really wasn't loyal to anything. After that I practiced Zen Buddhism."

> *Many different religious practices can be found among New Agers. In the general U.S. population, most of whom have no allegiance to the New Age Movement, almost one in four persons believe that astrology is a source for foretelling the future. Roughly the same number believe that crystals are a source for healing or energizing power and that tarot cards are a reliable source for making life decisions.*

From General New Ager to Astrology Specialist

Marcia's years of New Age experimentation continued when she moved to Atlanta after she graduated from college. She began spending time in Little Five Points, a countercultural hangout in Atlanta. In 1980 she learned that several New Age classes were being offered in the area. Marcia enrolled in two of the classes: psychic development and astrology.

"I had been spending years learning from other people about the endless offerings of New Age beliefs," she explained. "I was ready to learn about one area and become an expert."

She found that niche in her astrology class. "I realized that astrology was my thing, even though there is heavy math at the beginning," she recalled. "But I was willing to study hard to get to the parts that I really enjoyed."

Although we had known Marcia for just a few hours, we had already formed certain impressions. One clear impression I had was that she was intense in whatever path she journeyed. I could easily see her sacrificing hours of time to learn as much as possible about this segment of New Age beliefs.

"I kept taking more courses in astrology," she said. "Eventually, I decided to establish my own astrology practice. But in the city of Atlanta, you have to take a board certification exam in astrology, and you have to purchase a license." In 1983 Marcia passed the exam, bought the license, and started practicing professionally.

> Some of the common beliefs in the New Age Movement include monism, meaning that all that exists comes from a singular source of divine energy; pantheism, the belief that all that exists is God and that God is all that exists; reincarnation and karma; religious syncretism, the combination of many different religious and philosophical beliefs and practices; ecological centeredness and responsibility; and a belief in a new world order.

From Marcia's perspective at the time, the opportunity to have her own astrology practice was great timing. She had given birth to a son in 1981, and she desired to stay at home while her husband worked. His income was modest, so Marcia felt the financial pressure to provide a second income. The astrology endeavor allowed her to stay at home with her son and provide additional income.

She started reading charts during the day and delivering them to clients at night when her husband was at home. She became very good at reading charts and building a clientele. Her efforts were noticed by leaders of astrology in the community, and she was asked to serve on the Board of Astrology Examiners. This board was responsible for formulating the exam required to practice astrology. After one year on the board, she became chairperson, a position she held for the next three years.

Her practice continued to grow in the 1980s, and her name became well recognized by many in astrology. She often taught classes in astrology and became a regular writer for a New Age magazine. Her writing expanded her opportunities even more.

"I started doing charts for people on tape recorder and mailing them to the clients," she said with a laugh. "Clients even started purchasing my services as gifts to give others. My Southern Baptist mother promoted me to her friends and got me several new clients." Like many who dabble in horoscopes and astrology, her mother was not aware of the dangerous demonic presence in these practices.

One person who was not pleased with Marcia's work was her agnostic, antisupernatural father. "He asked me if I really believed what I was doing," Marcia recalled. "I was offended! I told him that I sure did believe it, that I wouldn't be spending so much time with something I didn't believe in."

Growth of Anti-Christian Sentiment

Marcia Montenegro's pilgrimage into the dark world of the occult and New Age deepened her dislike of Christianity. She was becoming more and more hostile not only to the beliefs of the Christian faith, but to Christians as well. Her feelings were affirmed by the televangelist scandals of the 1980s. She, like many of her New Age colleagues, anticipated the rapid decline of Christianity.

"We believed that the Age of Aquarius was on the horizon," she said as she sipped her beverage. "Christianity was on the decline and a new world order was near. I believed that Jesus was an advanced spiritual teacher. His birth initiated the Age of Pisces. He taught humanity love and compassion."

> The term New Age originated in the 1950s and is a utopian vision that describes a time of great harmony, human progress, and world government. It represents the end of wars, diseases, hunger, pollution, and poverty. There will be no allegiance to nations or tribes. Sometimes this new era is called the New World Order; other times it is called the Age of Aquarius. According to astrologers, Aquarians are visionary and open-minded. This new age is tied to this eleventh sign of the zodiac.

Marcia rejected with hostility orthodox Christian beliefs. God was not a personal being who sent his Son to die for humanity. "God was an energy force," she said of her past perspectives. "We all came from God, and God was in everything. I also believed in reincarnation."

Marcia's stature in the New Age community continued to grow, particularly among those in astrology. In 1989 she was elected president of the Metro Atlanta Astrological Society. Life seemed good. Her reputation was growing. Her clientele was increasing. And income from her astrological profession was good.

But God had other plans.

Every one of our stories in this book is truly an unexpected journey. Marcia Montenegro's story is no exception. She had no idea that the 1990s would usher in a radical shift in her beliefs. And she had no idea that she would soon embrace the Savior she had rejected for so many years.

A Waterfall of Love

The days were getting warmer in Atlanta in the spring of 1990. In the midst of a busy astrology schedule, Marcia began having strange thoughts and feelings. She could not explain why she began to have a compulsion to attend a church. It made no sense. She didn't believe in the God of the Christians, and she resented Christianity and Christians themselves. Why would she be having such thoughts about church?

But the thoughts and feelings would not abate. Marcia had believed for years that she had been a Christian in a previous life. That would be the only explanation for an otherwise inexplicable situation.

Finally, in the summer of 1990, Marcia made a reticent decision. She would attend a church. She chose a large Episcopalian congregation that she had noticed earlier. On the next Sunday, she made a bold step. She entered the church and sat quietly, if not resentfully, near the back of the sanctuary.

The clergy and choir entered the sanctuary in a celebratory procession. Leading everyone was a young boy carrying a cross. "When he passed by me," Marcia said softly, "I began to weep. I couldn't explain it. What I felt was total love overwhelming me. It was like a waterfall of love."

Marcia has no doubt today that she experienced the love of Christ reaching out to her. "It was very powerful and very, very real. I knew even then that God was personal and that he loved me. I couldn't stop crying."

She went back the next Sunday to the church and soon became a regular guest. "Eventually I got comfortable enough to tell people at the church that I was an astrologer," she said. "No one seemed to be bothered; some were actually interested. I thought that this was cool; I might even get some clients from the church."

Marcia was invited to attend a confirmation class even though she had no idea what it was. "They would start explaining things about the church," she chuckled, "and I would tell them about Zen Buddhism. Nobody seemed to mind; they were very open."

Despite the open-mindedness of those at the church, Marcia could not dispel a nagging feeling that astrology was wrong. "I wasn't a Christian, but I had more conviction against astrology than the church members did," she lamented. "I just had a sense that God didn't like astrology."

She made an appointment with the rector and told him pointedly about her convictions. "He told me," Marcia recalled, 'When you have Christ, you don't need astrology.' I left with the miserable certainty that I would have to stop."

> Although no numbers can be stated with certainty, an estimated 10 to 15 million Americans are active New Age participants. Another 20 to 30 million people in the United States are interested or are dabbling in New Age beliefs and practices.

Giving Up Astrology before Believing in Christ

"This was no small decision for me," Marcia told us. "I was on four key astrology committees. I was teaching astrology classes. I was writing articles in New Age magazines. And I had this job where I did office work part of the time, but my main purpose was to read charts of the employees for my boss. The employees didn't know that was the reason I was there, but it was a key source of income for me."

I interjected, "You were looking at giving up your income and your livelihood."

Marcia responded soberly, "It was far more than that. Astrology was my identity and meaning for life."

But Marcia made the traumatic decision. When clients called to ask for a reading of their charts, Marcia declined, stating courteously that she was taking a break from astrology. She had many friends in the pagan community, particularly witches. She explained to them that she was not reading charts anymore. She told her boss that she could no longer do charts on employees. "I had already been paid to do a few charts, so I did them," she recalled. "But in December 1990 I did my last chart, and I never returned to astrology."

Marcia's initial hopes when she first started attending the Episcopal church was that she could mix astrology with Christianity. And though no one told her otherwise, she sensed that the two beliefs were incompatible. Amazingly, all these developments transpired when she was not even a follower of Christ.

But that was about to change as well.

Marcia Meets Christ

The restaurant was quiet now. The lunch traffic was gone; the few remaining patrons were getting coffee or cappuccinos to escape the chilling rain. Marcia paused and took a sip from her own cup. I looked at my plate and realized that I had consumed the entirety of my meal. I really wondered what I had eaten. I didn't think my wife would tell me if I asked.

Nellie Jo and I were in our tenth *Journey* interview, but we never grew weary of hearing these astounding conversion stories. We waited for Marcia to resume because we knew the most important part of her story was imminent.

"I wasn't sure where to turn next," she continued. "So I decided to start reading the Bible. I can't explain why I chose to begin in the New Testament; it just seemed the right thing to do, so I started in Matthew. There was just something about reading the Bible. The words just seemed so pure.

"I got to Matthew 8 and read the story of Jesus on the sea [Matthew 8:23–27]. When I read the part where Jesus rebukes and calms the sea and the wind, it was like a light went on, like a fog lifted.

"For the first time I saw who Jesus was. He was my Savior. I was a sinner and he would forgive my sins. Maybe my childhood exposure to the Bible helped me to understand some of this, but I know in December 1990 Jesus became very real to me. I realized that I needed Jesus. I gave my life to him, and I realized all that other spiritual stuff that I had been involved in for so many years was totally false."

Marcia returned to the confirmation class at the Episcopal church. "I tried to explain to them what had happened to me," she told us, "but they didn't seem to understand."

First Steps as a Christian

Marcia Montenegro was now a follower of Jesus Christ. She found joy and peace in her Savior immediately, but life still had its obstacles. "I began to lose all my friends because all of my relationships were tied up with people who held New Age beliefs. I needed Christian friends."

Of course, the obvious place to find those friends was at the church. "The confirmation class was having a retreat to complete the confirmation process," she told us. "We were in the beautiful mountains of North Georgia. Two disturbing events made me leave the class."

The first event took place when she heard some of the Christian leaders say that adultery is okay sometimes. "Even though I was a new Christian," Marcia exclaimed, "I knew how off-base they were."

The second event was a conversation with a retired bishop who was leading the adult confirmation class. "He happened to mention to me," Marcia said, "that after the class he was going to Scotland. I asked him where he was going in Scotland, and he told me it was a small town that I probably wouldn't recognize. But I pressed him, and he said he was going to Findhorn."

Marcia was flabbergasted. "I looked at him and said, 'Findhorn! That's one of the biggest New Age communities in the world!' He looked and me and asked, 'Do you think the New Age conflicts with Christianity?' I told him, 'I sure do. That's what God saved me from.' He walked away without speaking."

> The key difference between classic Hindu beliefs on reincarna-
> tion and New Age reincarnation is that Hindus believe the
> human soul can return as a lower life-form, while New Age
> proponents believe in upward mobility in reincarnation.

Not all of Marcia's experiences as a new Christian were negative. "There was this real nice guy in my office named Jeff," she
recalled. "About four months after I became a Christian, I told him
that I was saved after years of practicing astrology. He said, 'Maybe
someone was praying for you.' I told him that no one would have
been praying for me.

"He began to smile, and then I realized that he was speaking
of himself. But he wasn't by himself. His Bible study group had
been praying for me for a year. Can you imagine that? An entire
group of young adults praying for my salvation for a whole year.
That was so incredible."

Advice from a Former New Ager

"How can we be effective witnesses to the millions who hold some
New Age beliefs?" I asked Marcia.

"First," she said, "I would advise Christians to stop making
fun of New Agers. Every Christian seems to have a joke about
Shirley MacLaine. Christians will get nowhere with sarcastic
stereotypes."

She continued, "Next, I would try to find out what they
believe. The New Age Movement is so diverse. I would ask them
what their spiritual path is. If you can engage them in conversation, you will probably have many opportunities to share what you
believe. But you have to be willing to listen."

Marcia also recommended that Christians understand basic
apologetic issues. "New Agers," she said, "like anyone who is not
a Christian, have a lot of questions, and they are usually going to
ask some of the tough questions. You have to be ready to respond."

Marcia reminded us again about one of the key issues we had heard in many of our interviews. "You really have to love these people," she insisted. "They will know if you have a true spirit of caring or not. If you do, they will probably be willing to talk and to listen. Every one of them has something missing in their lives. They need to hear about the waterfall of love that Jesus poured over me."

The rain had stopped outside. For the first time that day, we were beginning to see some sunshine. In some ways the weather pattern again seemed symbolic of the story we had just heard. A lengthy period of darkness and storms was followed by calm and a bright light.

Marcia's son is a follower of Christ. Marcia's sister became a Christian at almost the same time as Marcia. And their parents were both saved prior to their deaths. The hope of eternal life spreads from one family member to another.

We said our good-byes and got into our cars. Nellie Jo and I both were smiling. The sunlight was now shining brightly on both of us. What a difference the light makes.

In just a few days we would meet with another *Journey* traveler, a former Muslim with yet another remarkable story. For now we enjoyed the drive back to Virginia Beach. God's waterfall of love had touched us all.

CHAPTER ELEVEN

"MY HATRED OF WHITE CHRISTIANS LED ME TO IT"

FROM BLACK MUSLIM TO TRADITIONAL ISLAM TO CHRISTIANITY

November 9
Louisville, Kentucky

I shared in the acknowledgments of this book about the heartbreaking diagnosis of Nellie Jo's cancer. You also read about my own surgery during the research and interviews for this project. I could share further with you other personal challenges Nellie Jo and I faced in the year we worked on this book, but that would distract from the message of *The Unexpected Journey*.

Yet I must admit that I wondered at times if we were meeting the opposition of the Evil One in our attempts to bring this book to fruition. I will not dwell on that issue, for that question cannot be answered on this side of eternity.

What I do know is that the conversations we heard point to a powerful and sovereign God and his glory. Satan cannot be pleased with the glorious conversion stories we were privileged to hear. I do know that the faith of Nellie Jo and myself has been strengthened by this journey. In the midst of our personal trials, we have learned to trust the God of all hope even more.

Our eleventh interview is a clear case of a powerful God reaching out in hope and love. The story you are about to hear is the journey of a bitter African American who found identity with the Black Muslims. You will also hear about his journey to traditional Islam and finally to Jesus Christ.

As I intersperse explanations of his beliefs in this chapter, you will note that I begin with the beliefs of the Black Muslims and then move on to Islam. Such was the journey of a poor black sharecropper named Robert Moseley.

Meet Mumin Muhammad, Formerly Robert Moseley

The institution where I serve as dean, the Southern Baptist Theological Seminary, is one of the largest seminaries in the world, with more than four thousand students. I wish I could get to know all of them, but that is not possible. Many of them have stories of extraordinary journeys.

Dr. George Martin, who serves as associate dean and professor of missions at the seminary, heard about my research for this book. A man never without an opinion, George urged me to interview Mumin Muhammad to hear his story of being both a Black Muslim and a traditional Muslim. After screening several potential candidates, I saw the wisdom of George's insights. I hope he doesn't read this chapter; I would hate to admit to him that he was right.

Nellie Jo and I had the opportunity to relax a few more days at home since our conversation would be with someone from Louisville. On a mild fall day, the three of us met in a Starbucks on the east side of town.

Mumin Muhammad walked into Starbucks with a smile on his face. He humbly expressed the honor he had of being a part of this project. We would soon discover that the privilege was all ours.

We once again experienced God's presence as we heard the powerful story of a man touched by the love of Christ.

Prejudice and Hatred

Mumin was born in 1948 near Columbus, Mississippi, as Robert Moseley. He never knew his father, and he was raised most of his youth by his grandparents. This African American spent his early years on a plantation owned by Anglos. When he was nine years old, his grandfather saved enough money to lease land from black sharecroppers. Because his family needed Robert to work in the fields, he was not able to begin school until he was nine years old. "I was a big kid in the first grade," he laughed loudly.

Mumin admitted that school was tough for him in many ways. "I didn't get any help in my education at home," he told us. "Neither of my grandparents could read or write. They couldn't even sign their names."

But school was tough for other reasons. "Our schools were totally segregated," Mumin recalled. "I never had a conversation with a white person until I was twenty-one years old. The Ku Klux Klan was all over the place. I got beaten with the butt of a gun one time because I said 'yes' instead of 'yes, sir,' to a white man at a gas station."

Mumin told us several other stories of abuse and prejudice he experienced as a child. I felt my eyes welling with tears. I was going back to my own childhood where I had witnessed many of the atrocities of which he spoke.

Mumin's grandparents were faithful churchgoing Christians, and they took their grandchild to church on a regular basis. But the impressionable child was not convinced that the Christian faith was genuine. "I saw white people smiling and carrying Bibles on Sunday, and then they would beat us and call us niggers the rest of the week," Mumin sadly recalled.

Those racially explosive and abusive years were having their effect on Mumin. "By the time I was in junior high school, I was already reading about Black Muslims and the Black Panthers," he told us. A radical change in his life was about to take place. Robert would soon become Mumin.

Black Muslims Reach Out

The transition seemed very natural to the young African American. "As soon as I finished high school, I joined the Black Muslims," he stated matter-of-factly. "A professor at the junior college helped me to become a part of the growing movement."

"What was your primary motivation for joining?" I asked naively.

"My hatred of white Christians led me to Black Muslims," he responded, looking down. "The Black Muslims offered me an identity and a way to vent my anger against white people." He changed his name from Robert Moseley to Mumin Muhammad.

> Black Muslims are an African-American religious movement founded in 1930 in Detroit by Wali Farad, whom his followers believed to be Allah in person. Farad mysteriously disappeared in 1934. He was succeeded by Elijah Muhammad, who moved the headquarters of the movement from Detroit to Chicago.

"The only Jesus I knew was the white Jesus with blue eyes and blonde hair, the Jesus sung about by members of the Klan. I just saw too much hypocrisy in the white man's religion," Mumin said.

"When I became a Black Muslim, I had an identity. I was absorbed by their culture. Now, looking back, I realize that I wasted thirty years of my life in a religion that enslaved me just like whites once enslaved the blacks."

That comment brought an awkward silence to our table for a moment.

Mumin then continued. "I was a loyal Black Muslim. I worked for them tirelessly, often giving my entire earnings to the movement. I was seeking to be somebody, to have an identity that meant something," he reflected.

> One of the better known of the Black Muslims was Malcolm X (Malcolm Little), who served as minister under Elijah Muhammad. Tensions developed between the two leaders, and Malcolm X was suspended in 1963 and then formed his own organization. He was assassinated in 1965.

"But I also saw some of the good things Black Muslims were doing," Mumin countered. "They helped people get off drugs. They took indigents off welfare. They helped alcoholics recover and got prostitutes off the street. Black Muslims taught self-respect and self-worthiness."

Mumin's faithfulness and work ethic began to pay off. "I started off as an FOI, which literally means 'fruit of Islam.' An FOI is a foot soldier willing to do anything for the cause. I worked a paper route and gave all my money to the organization.

"I then was promoted to sergeant, then to lieutenant, and finally to a minister. I became one of the spokesmen for Black Muslims, preaching out of the Chicago headquarters."

Mumin was not just another religious minister. He became the assistant minister to the new leader of Black Muslims, Wallace Muhammad. Many opportunities awaited him in his new leadership role.

> When Elijah Muhammad died in 1975, he was succeeded by his son, Wallace Muhammad. Wallace started preaching a less inflammatory form of Islam. He also aligned the movement with the international Islamic community, moving toward Sunni Islamic practices.

Rising in the Black Muslim Movement

Mumin followed the Black Muslim movement in its stronger ties with the Arab world. The name of the organization was changed to the World Community of Islam in the West and later to the American Society of Muslims. He was fast becoming an adherent of the more traditional Muslim beliefs.

> Islam has humble beginnings. Muhammad ibn Abdallah was sitting in a cave outside Mecca in A.D. 610 when he began to receive visions from what he believed to be the archangel Gabriel. The angel declared that there was only one true God; Muhammad spoke of him as "Allah," a name that simply means "the God."

Mumin took the opportunity of taking the dream trip of every Muslim. He made the pilgrimage (called the *hajj*) to Mecca in Saudi Arabia. To Muslims, the hajj demonstrates the global unity of Islam and the equality of everyone before Allah. Millions of Muslims make the pilgrimage each year. While in Saudi Arabia Mumin was invited by King Fahid to the palace. He sat at the king's table for an unforgettable dinner.

"When I returned to Chicago after the hajj," Mumin told us, "I was more passionate about my religion than ever. It became my goal to convert as many Americans to Islam as possible. I wanted to see more mosques in the United States than churches."

Mumin also continued to serve as an assistant minister to Wallace Muhammad. Under his leadership the ties to the Arabic world grew even stronger. Mumin also married, started back to college, and began serving as an imam, which would have some parallels in the Christian world to a minister or pastor.

"I was fully into Islam," Mumin told us. "I led in worship and spiritual services. I led in prayer. I really felt like Islam was the only true religion."

But God would soon place events in Mumin's life that would erode his certainty about Islam. A new journey toward Christ had begun.

> In 1977 a group of Black Muslims led by Louis Farrakhan split from the organization and started an organization called the Nation of Islam. In the late 1990s this group also began to embrace more traditional Islamic practices. In 2000, Farrakhan and Wallace Muhammad publicly declared an end to the rivalry between the two groups.

Questions and Uncertainty

"I was attending a college in downtown Chicago," Mumin resumed. "The president called me into his office and presented me with an opportunity to take a world tour. I would be with other college students of many other religions. I remember they included Jews, Hindus, Christians, Muslims, New Agers, and many more.

"They offered to pay all of our expenses as we traveled around the world together. Ironically, the trip was funded by the Moonies. I jumped at the offer.

> Islam is the second largest of the world's religions, with more than 1 billion adherents. It is also the youngest of the major world religions.

"I have trouble remembering all the places we went," Mumin smiled. "I remember stops in Egypt, Israel, Italy, the Vatican, China, India, and Nepal. I'm probably missing some."

But it was the journey to Israel that impacted Mumin the greatest. "I was able to go to many different places in Israel," he said, "but I remember most clearly going to the place where they said Jesus was born. I was already beginning to ask myself questions when I was with these young people from so many different beliefs. How did I know that I had the truth in Islam?"

Mumin also began to recall that he did not originally join the Black Muslims for what they believed. He mostly wanted to be a part of a group with which he found identity and purpose. He had never really questioned the beliefs of the Black Muslims or the more traditional forms of Islam.

"When I was at the purported birthplace of Jesus," Mumin spoke softly, "I prayed to God that he would show me the truth. I said something like, 'Lord, if I am wrong, help me to see truth.' I was really sensing that something was wrong."

Nellie Jo asked Mumin if his prayer was a Muslim prayer.

"No," he said quietly, "it was a prayer of the heart. I just knew something was wrong."

The Journey to Christ

When Mumin returned to Chicago in 1985, his fellow Muslims began to notice something different about him. "They said I had lost my commitment and my zeal," he said with a somber expression. "They began to question me. I started attending less and less; I was gradually breaking away. But the Black Muslims were not happy with me. Some of them began to threaten my life."

When we first asked Mumin to consider participating in *The Unexpected Journey* project, we offered him anonymity. We had already had initial conversations with other former Muslims. Some of them did fear that harm would come to them if they participated in this book. But Mumin elected to reveal his true name. He declined our offer of anonymity with a simple shrug and a few words about trusting God. He also told us that the militant and deadly Muslims that get most of the attention represent a very small percentage of all Muslims.

Mumin reminded us that at this point in his journey he was a married man with three children. "They didn't know anything but Islam. And I just stopped associating myself with the Muslims. "By early 1986," he told us, "I had completely withdrawn myself from fellowship."

> Islam holds to five major doctrines. The first doctrine is the belief in one all-knowing and all-powerful God. Allah loves those he deems to be good. (By contrast, the God of the Bible loves humans even in their sinful state.) Second, Islam holds to a hierarchy of created beings. Angels are between humans and Allah. Third, Muslims have a sacred book called the Qur'an. Fourth, Islam is a prophetic religion. Some of the better-known prophets, according to Islam, are Adam, Noah, Abraham, Moses, David, Solomon, Jonah, John the Baptist, and Jesus. Fifth, Muslims hold to the belief that physical death is not the end of life. Those whose good deeds outweigh the bad deeds go to heaven. The others go to a place of eternal suffering. Thus salvation, unlike Christianity, is based on works.

During this period of doubt and spiritual wandering, Mumin was invited to a Baptist church on the west side of Chicago. "I was thirty-nine years old," Mumin chuckled, "and I had not been in a church since junior high school. But here I was going to a Baptist church and taking my Muslim wife and my three Muslim kids."

Nellie Jo and I did not ask Mumin how his family reacted to his insistence that they go to a Baptist church with him. We can only imagine that it was an interesting conversation.

"When the preacher started preaching, I was focused like a laser," Mumin continued. "He shared the gospel so clearly—about sin, about who Jesus is, about repentance and faith. And he shared that salvation is a free gift for those who place their faith in Christ."

There was a momentary pause. I think Nellie Jo and I were almost holding our breaths.

Mumin slammed his hand on the table. "That did it!" he exclaimed. "I knew then that I needed Jesus."

His abrupt movement caused me to jump. I asked for a brief break.

When I returned to the table, Mumin resumed his story as if I had never left. "The pastor offered a public invitation, and I went forward. He asked why I had come forward, and I told him I had accepted Jesus and wanted to join the church. He then asked me my name. When I told him I was Mumin Muhammad, I thought he was going to choke. He couldn't believe it."

I asked Mumin about his family's reaction. "They all thought I was crazy," he laughed in recollection. "They thought I had cracked and lost my mind."

Although I would never suggest that this moment in Mumin's life was anything but a remarkable and sobering experience, I had to admit to myself that it had a bit of humor in it. A leader in the Muslim community for thirty years walks into a Baptist church with his Muslim family and accepts Christ. The pastor is rendered speechless, and the family thinks their husband and father has lost his mind.

Difficult Days in Discipleship

Inevitably in our interviews we heard that becoming a Christian did not cause all of one's problems to disappear. Such was the case with Mumin. He faced some serious family problems in the midst of his newfound faith.

> Islam is different from Christianity in the Muslim repudiation of the doctrine of the Trinity. Also, Islam does not view Jesus Christ as divine. Interestingly, however, Jesus Christ is believed to be a sinless prophet, but Muhammad is not regarded as such.

Mumin's first challenge was the offer of a job transfer from Chicago to St. Louis. "I felt I really needed to get out of Chicago," he told us, "but my wife and kids did not want to leave Chicago."

He eventually made the decision to move without them, with plans to come home every weekend.

Mumin worked in St. Louis from 1986 to 1989. He did not miss a weekend back with his family in Chicago. But the weekday separation and the differences in spiritual beliefs began to take their toll, straining the marriage.

Another issue with which Mumin struggled was his name. Should he revert back to his non-Muslim name? How would his family react since they knew him by no other name than Mumin Muhammad?

He sought counsel from a Baptist pastor. Both men weighed the benefits of each option. They decided that it was best for him to keep his Muslim name. "I knew there would be opportunities where my name could be used to share Christ," he explained.

But the new Christian really needed some ongoing discipleship. In his hectic dual life in two cities, he was not able to get involved in a church with consistency or to have regular fellowship with other Christians. Mumin describes this period as a "test of faith." He had moments of doubt about his conversion and about Jesus. He knew something had to change.

The Former Muslim Goes to Church

Mumin convinced his wife to move to St. Louis in 1989, three years after his move. The first week the family was in town, he told his wife that he had found a church for the family to attend. She asked what kind of church it was, and he told her it was Southern Baptist.

"My wife said, 'You've got to be crazy.' She showed me an article that explained the beginning of Southern Baptists, where it split from its former denomination because they wanted slave owners to be able to be missionaries. Here I was a former Black Muslim going to a church in a denomination founded on issues of slavery."

"Did your wife go with you?" Nellie Jo asked.

"No, but she allowed the kids to go," Mumin responded. "They didn't like it at first, but they started getting involved in the youth programs. They soon fell in love with the church. Even my wife appreciated the alternative activities for kids. My children started waking me up on Sundays to go to church!"

> Among the good deeds Muslims must perform are five major acts called the Five Pillars of Faith. The first pillar is the daily and public recitation of the Shahadah: "There is no God but Allah, and Muhammad is his messenger." Second, prayers must be offered five times a day. A third pillar is the giving of alms in the amount of 2.5 percent of one's income. Fourth, regular fasting is expected of Muslims. And the fifth pillar is the pilgrimage to Mecca called the hajj.

But Mumin's marriage continued to deteriorate. He requested and received a transfer back to Illinois, hoping that returning to his wife's home would heal the marriage. Sadly, nothing seemed to work. They separated in 1997 and divorced in 1999.

I could see the pain on Mumin's face as he told us the story of his marriage. His new faith had cost him greatly.

Then his face brightened. "Three years after our divorce," Mumin began, "my wife accepted Christ. I have never dated since our divorce. Now my wife and I have a friendship that is stronger than at any point in our marriage. I am taking it slowly, but I am praying that the Lord will reunite us. She has become such a beautiful Christian with a great testimony."

I could feel the lump in my throat as Mumin expressed his lingering deep love for his ex-wife. I looked across the table at my bride of twenty-seven years and thanked God for such a wonderful gift.

> One exception allows Muslims to enter into heaven without having their deeds judged. Those who die martyrs in defense of the Islamic faith in a holy war (called a jihad) avoid the uncertain outcome of seeing how their deeds stack up.

Ever the mama, Nellie Jo asked the next question. "What has happened to your children spiritually?"

Mumin grinned in response. "I have seen all of them come to faith in the Lord Jesus Christ. My oldest son became a Christian in 1990. My middle son accepted Christ in 1994, and my daughter became a Christian in 2003. Now my whole family follows Jesus!"

"What is your attitude today toward white people?" I asked next.

"That was one of the great things Jesus did in my life," Mumin responded. "When I realized what he did in forgiving me by dying on the cross, I learned how to forgive those who had persecuted me and called me a nigger. Being able to forgive is a great gift of my salvation."

> Islam contains several different sects, but the two largest are the Shiites and the Sunnis. The Shiites split from the larger Islamic community over the issue of leadership. They believe that the successor of Muhammad should be of his bloodline. They are dominant in Iran, Iraq, Lebanon, and parts of Africa. The Sunnis believe that leaders should be elected and that religion and government should be separate. Sunnis account for almost 80 percent of the Muslim population and are heavily represented in Egypt, Saudi Arabia, and Pakistan.

A Former Muslim on Reaching Muslims

"You have been a leader among the Black Muslims and the more traditional Islamic community," I said rhetorically. "How can we reach Muslims for Christ in America today?"

Mumin stated the obvious first: "It is extremely hard." Then he added, "In God's power it can be done.

"First, Christians must be grounded in their own faith. A Christian who does not spend time in the Word is no match for a Muslim. But you can't be intimidated by Muslims. I was a

Muslim who was lost and needed Christ. I needed to hear the gospel."

We were reminded that Mumin responded positively the first time his wife's cousin invited him to church. "Many Christians today are just afraid to invite a Muslim to church," Mumin stated. "You never know how God might be working in their lives."

"You have to have some people in each church who know Islam well," Mumin said. "While every Christian should know the basics of Islam, different people should specialize in different faiths in each church. I would like to see many churches develop a department of apologetics to reach different groups."

I nodded. I really liked that idea.

"Christians need to be willing to establish relationships with Muslims," Mumin continued. "We need to make the sacrifice to get to know them well and listen to them. We would have many opportunities to share our beliefs."

Mumin paused for a moment. "We must show genuine compassion and concern for Muslims," he said with emphasis. "They will know if we are showing genuine love. Muslims are doing a much better job of reaching African Americans in prison than Christians are. They are giving them hope and identity. Where are all the Christians willing to make such sacrifices and offer true hope and identity in Christ?"

Mumin's question did not have to be answered. We all knew what needed to be done.

I closed our conversation by asking Mumin how we could pray for him. His response is worth repeating.

"Pray for me," he said, "that my life will be used for God's glory. I want to make a difference. I was a follower of the Devil for many years of my life. I followed a false god and a false doctrine. Pray that I will serve the one true God with greater service and fervency than I ever did serving a false god as a Muslim."

So we prayed. And Nellie Jo and I knew that God was already answering that prayer in Mumin's life even before we prayed it.

I saw a friend, Tom Harper, at another table in Starbucks. He asked me about the long conversation we had been having. I simply told Tom that we were hearing the story of a modern-day miracle. Muslims can be reached for Christ, I said. Muslims can respond to Christian love.

On the way out, I got a tall white chocolate mocha, convincing myself that only a few calories could be in such a small cup. I said parting words to Mumin. As he walked toward his car, I spoke softly to my wife, "There goes a miracle. Look what God has done."

The Unexpected Journey was almost complete. The last leg of the journey would take place in just a few days in Augusta, Georgia. A former satanist would tell us yet another amazing story. I wanted to hear the story, but in many ways I did not want this journey to end.

I hugged my wife when we got in the car. One more interview, I told her. She nodded. We had seen twelve changed lives, but we both knew another reality. Our lives had been changed as well. That miraculous hope that we had witnessed again and again would prepare us for our own difficult journey ahead.

CHAPTER TWELVE

"I EXPERIENCED THE POWER OF THE SATANIC REALM"

THE UNEXPECTED JOURNEY FROM SATAN TO JESUS

November 11
Augusta, Georgia

In many ways I was not looking forward to this day. Nellie Jo and I had no idea what to expect when interviews for *The Unexpected Journey* began. We did know, however, that any expectations had been greatly exceeded. We had many conversations about changed lives, and ours had been changed by listening to these inspiring stories.

And now the last conversation was about to begin. We really did not want it to be over. I kidded with my wife that I hoped this book would outsell all of my previous works. When she asked why, I smiled and said that I would be ready to travel again to write a sequel. She agreed.

With late fall temperatures dropping in Louisville, we were both looking forward to traveling south. Unfortunately, the Deep South was experiencing a cold snap, and the temperatures were not much better than Louisville.

We flew to Columbia, South Carolina, and drove to Augusta, Georgia, because the Columbia flight was much more affordable than flying into Augusta. We had an appointment in Augusta with Jeff Harshbarger and his wife, Liz.

My wife was reading through the file that my secretary, Kathy Fredrick, had prepared for our trip. I asked Nellie Jo where we were to meet with Jeff and Liz. "A restaurant," she responded with a mischievous smile.

"What kind of restaurant?" I asked with dreadful anticipation.

"Italian," she responded with the same smile.

I was silent for the next five minutes, thinking once again how I was about to be deprived of my three major food groups of meat, potatoes, and diet sodas.

Finally, Nellie Jo broke the silence.

"Look, most Italian restaurants let you design your own pizza. I'm sure you can get beef and lots of cheese."

I was a happy camper. Let the interview begin!

An Unlikely Looking Ex-Satanist

You would think after eleven interviews that I would learn not to stereotype people. But I was still surprised when Jeff and Liz walked into the restaurant. I'm not sure what I was expecting, maybe a black-hooded robe and blood-red eyes.

Jeff Harshbarger looked like the good guy next door. In fact, his wife commented that when he was younger and had long hair he looked like John Lennon, wire-rim glasses and all. Imagine.

Jeff and Liz lead Refuge Ministries in Augusta, a ministry that informs others about the dangers of satanism, the occult, and New Age beliefs, and provides help as well. A former satanist was about to tell us how he fell into the snares of the world of the occult, only to be rescued by the power of Jesus Christ.

Why Family Matters

Jeff Harshbarger was part of a large family that experienced many moves and tumultuous times. His earliest memories are of his family at Camp Lejeune in North Carolina where his father served as a marine sergeant. The family's next move was to Camp Pendleton in Southern California. His best childhood memories are in the warmth of Southern California sunshine.

When Jeff's father returned from Vietnam, he was a different man. "Nothing was the same after that," Jeff said sadly. "Several men serving with him were ambushed and killed. Dad began to drink when he returned home."

His father received an honorable discharge and expected benefits for his time in military service. For reasons Jeff does not fully understand, the benefits were never approved. His father became bitter and drank even more.

One of the early heartaches Jeff remembers was the family leaving California. "I remember, even though I was very young, seeing the palm trees of California disappear as I looked out the back window of the car. It was a sad time."

Jeff's father had found work in Indiana. But the drinking continued, and fights between Jeff's mother and father were frequent and furious. "I would just start crying in school all the time. I had to see a school therapist," Jeff said.

Jeff spent a significant amount of time in the interview talking about his family. He had a purpose in this aspect of our conversation. "Liz and I deal with young people who get involved in the occult all the time," he told us. "Some of the kids come from bad families. They are seeking to fill voids in their lives." Such is the reason Jeff became attracted to the world of the occult himself.

From Dabbling to Dangerous: The World of the Occult

The waitress had little help at the restaurant. We guessed that they had not expected many people in the middle of the afternoon, but the place was two-thirds full. Despite the heavy demands to serve all the tables, she did a very good job of taking care of us. The few times she ran a little slow, she apologized profusely. We all assured her that we understood and were fine with her service.

Jeff continued to share with us the difficulties of his family life. His father's drinking did not abate. His parents still fought. His father would move from town to town in Indiana. Jeff's family was moving every year.

"When I was in the third grade," Jeff recalled, "I would wake up in the middle of the night and feel a presence in the house. I really began to be curious about what was happening. I had no family to give me strength, so I was looking for something else in my life."

> Some people erroneously assign any occultist activities to satanism. In reality satanism is the worship of Satan in either a literal or a figurative form. Atheistic satanists worship the ideals of Satan but do not believe he is a real and personal figure. Theistic satanists see Satan as a literal figure, a deity who is the object of their worship.

Nellie Jo's hot tea arrived and Jeff resumed his story.

"The year I began to sense a presence in my house, I pulled out the family Ouija board," Jeff said. "I had always been suspicious that my brother moved the oracle, but he never owned up to it."

This time Jeff tried the Ouija board on his own. "I was going to prove that the oracle could not move on its own, but when I touched it, it moved," Jeff recalled.

"It scared me, but it was exciting too," he said energetically. "It was like being on a roller coaster. You are screaming in fear, but when it's over, you want to do it again. I was too young to know exactly what was happening to me, but I knew it was something I wanted to find out more about."

> Satanic dabblers are usually adolescents who adopt some of the trappings of satanism. Many of them are bored and have feelings of inadequacy. They may embrace other forms of satanism, but most reject them as they get older. A few may attempt to get involved in some of the more popular forms of Satan worship, such as animal sacrifice and blood rituals, but these tend to be exceptions.

Just prior to one of the family's many moves within the state of Indiana, Jeff had an unusual dream. "I was in the fifth grade when this next unusual event took place in my life," he said. "I dreamed that I left my body and went to the house where we were moving."

Because Nellie Jo and I had arrived at the appointment early, we had already had our meal before the Harshbargers' arrival. They each had ordered a slice of pizza, but Jeff had not been able to eat because we kept asking him questions. I called a timeout to allow him to eat and to allow Nellie Jo and me an opportunity to speak with Liz and to hear her perspective on several issues.

Jeff finished his pizza. I couldn't wait to hear more of his story. "Okay Jeff," I said, "we left you in a dream floating out of your body and traveling to the house where you were about to move. Pick up there."

He took a swallow of his water, wiped his face, and continued the story.

"In the dream I saw all of the rooms in the house in detail," Jeff said. "Then when we moved to the house, it was just like the dream. Even though I was still young, I decided that I had to investigate what was going on in my life."

Nellie Jo wanted to know if the Harshbarger family had any Christian influences in their lives at this time.

"Some of us kids went to church when different people invited us, but we never went to church as a family together. And Mom and Dad kept on fighting."

"Tell us about some more of your paranormal experiences when you were young," I encouraged Jeff.

"In the same year that I had the out-of-body dream, I saw one of my Christmas gifts wrapped in the package under the tree," Jeff continued. "I could see all of the contents of the package. When I told my mom, she got mad because she thought I had steamed open the package. That was my cue never to talk about these powers I had."

He did try to involve a friend in testing his powers. "We got a deck of cards. He would hold the cards to his head, and I would guess the card. I got it right almost every time. He freaked out and went home," Jeff said, laughing.

> Most of the satanists who have any formal affiliation with a group belong to the Church of Satan. Ironically, this group does not believe in the literal existence of Satan. One of their core beliefs is individual determinism, that individuals are purely responsible for their own actions.

Angry at the World and Open to Satan

"By the time in I was in the sixth grade, I had my purpose in life," Jeff reflected. "I was going to be the next Jeanne Dixon, the psychic who was so famous in the 70s. I was fascinated with ESP, the paranormal world, anything that would help me with this power I had."

But in the seventh grade, Jeff received a significant blow to any esteem he had left. "I was placed in a class of social misfits," he remembered sadly. "Because of my family problems, I was labeled. I got angry, and then I got depressed. I tried to hang out with higher caliber social groups, but they wouldn't accept me."

Jeff once again retreated from social contact and started studying the paranormal intensely. He read every book on the subject in the small town's library, some of them more than once.

By the time Jeff was in high school, he was in complete rebellion. He became drunk for the first time in the ninth grade and stayed drunk for three days. He attempted to find identity with the party crowd and the athletes, but nothing was working.

> *The Satanic Bible is a modern book written in the 1960s by Anton LaVey, the founder of the Church of Satan. Not a typical religious book, it espouses LaVey's personal philosophies rather than traditional satanic beliefs.*

The Italian restaurant had some great background music. Music of the 1960s and early 1970s is my favorite, and I sure was enjoying James Taylor crooning "You've Got a Friend" as I listened to Jeff.

When Jeff resumed his story, he fast-forwarded to his senior year of high school. He was not getting along well with his mother at home, and he could not wait to get out of the house.

During his senior year, he took a part-time job at a department store. The assistant manager of the store "was one of the coolest guys I had ever known," Jeff told us. "He really seemed to have his act together."

One afternoon in 1977 while he was working, a major snowstorm hit the small Indiana town. Jeff could not get home, and no one, not even his family, would come get him. The assistant manger of the store offered for Jeff to stay at his apartment.

"I remember thinking, 'Yes!'" Jeff recalled. "I was going to get to be a part of this guy's life that I thought was the coolest guy in the world."

They walked the short distance to his apartment in the storm. "When we opened the door and turned on the light," Jeff said with an almost melodramatic effect, "the first thing I saw was a ceramic skull with a candle in it.

"I began to look around the room. Everything in it seemed to have some paranormal or dark connection. I remember telling him, 'This is interesting.' Then I asked him what it was all about.

"He asked me if I was interested in what all this meant. I told him I was interested. Then he asked me how interested I was. I told him I was very interested. Then he said it without a blink: 'I am a satanist.'"

Jeff paused for a moment and sipped his water. "So I asked what that meant," Jeff continued. "And he told me that by being a satanist he had the philosophy and power to be in total control of his life. He then asked me, 'So you want to join?'"

In many ways, the events of most of Jeff's life seemed to be leading to this moment. "I had no identity, and this offered me identity," Jeff said. "I was mad at God, and this offered me a way to get back at God. I needed some way to see these powers in my life used, and this offered me the way to use those powers."

So when the friend asked if Jeff wanted to join, Jeff responded quickly. "Yeah, that sounds like something I would buy into."

That evening they had a ceremony in the apartment. "He initiated me," Jeff said. "He laid hands on me. I dedicated my soul and life to Satan. I experienced the power of the satanic realm."

In many ways Jeff thought he found his home and life. "It was both frightening and exciting. I no longer felt so alone. Now I had a sense of belonging."

Life as a Satanist

"My friend became my teacher," Jeff said. "He personally discipled me. We moved out of town and got new jobs. Christians were driving me crazy by witnessing to me in this town."

But Jeff did recall one witnessing encounter that was not so negative. "Our water heater broke in the house we were renting," he said. "The landlord came to fix it, and he started telling me about Jesus. But there was something different about him. Unlike all the others, he really seemed to care about me."

The reason Jeff told us that particular story would become evident near the conclusion of the interview. He is convinced that satanists, witches, New Agers, or anyone who is not a Christian will respond positively to true Christian concern and love. Unfortunately, few Christians are even willing to spend time with such persons.

> *The Satanic Bible has nine major statements:*
>
> 1. *Satan represents indulgence.*
> 2. *Satan represents vital existence, not pipe dreams.*
> 3. *Satan represents undefiled wisdom.*
> 4. *Satan represents kindness to those who deserve it.*
> 5. *Satan represents vengeance, instead of turning the other cheek.*
> 6. *Satan represents responsibility of the individual.*
> 7. *Satan represents man as just another animal.*
> 8. *Satan represents all the so-called sins that lead to gratification.*
> 9. *Satan is the best friend of the church, since it keeps the church in business.*

Jeff was not satisfied with the philosophical satanism he was practicing. He told his teacher, "Let's go for some real power." The friend and teacher agreed.

"We started going after the black arts," Jeff resumed. "We went from being philosophical satanists to true devil worshipers. We would do a ritual to be filled and possessed, and we really began to see results."

But Jeff and his friend were not content to hoard this new-found power to themselves. "We started to 'evangelize' others to become devil worshipers. We would have parties. And we would offer these teenagers the opportunity to join us in devil worship."

Soon the house was filled with eight persons, as six teenagers joined the new coven. "These were kids from some of the best families in town," Jeff told us. "I really began to care for these kids we had brought into our house."

> *Very few satanists see Satan as Christians do. He is not seen to be a force of evil, deceit, or destruction. Nor is he seen as a fallen angel as is depicted in the Christian Bible.*

All the young men in the coven decided to go to college together. But Jeff was not doing well. He had sought power, relationships, and meaning. And he thought he had found them in satanism. Instead, he found himself sinking deeper and deeper into depression.

"I was so tired of this inner turmoil in my life," Jeff said. "I was twenty-one years old, and nothing had worked in my life. I was so tired of the conflict. I just wanted it to be over."

Jeff bought a gun and a pint of whiskey. He checked into the Holiday Inn and prepared to kill himself.

The Turning Point

He sat in the motel room and drank his whiskey and smoked his pot. He was ready. He put the gun to his head—but he could not pull the trigger.

"I kept having this thought go through my head," Jeff said, "that was asking me where I was going to spend eternity. Why should that matter? I was going to hell to be with my lord and savior, Satan. Hell was my reward."

Jeff did not shoot himself. The following day he went to his home, rifle in hand. The members of his coven looked at him but said nothing. Jeff's mentor tried to cheer him up by having a party, but Jeff would have nothing to do with him. Soon all the "friends" left him alone as they went to find other parties.

Alone again, Jeff tried a second time to kill himself. "I went into the garage and got a rope. I made a noose on one end and tied the other end to the rafters. I stood on a chair and then kicked the chair from underneath my feet. I fell to the ground on hard concrete. I had two unsuccessful attempts at suicide. I couldn't even die."

> According to Adherents.com, the number of satanists depends on whom you ask. Some estimates are as high as 20,000; others are as low as 3,000. Satanists tend to socialize with each other via the Internet, in chat rooms and on message boards and websites.

Exhausted physically and emotionally, Jeff went to bed. "I cried like a baby," he said. Then I heard a voice that said, 'Get out.' I waited, expecting to see a demon at the foot of my bed. Instead, I heard the voice again: 'Get out.'"

Jeff opened his window. He was on the first floor, so he climbed outside through his window. "I stepped into the presence of God," he recalled with emotion. "I fell on my face and began to cry to God: 'Jesus, make my life okay. I'm giving in, Lord. I'm done.'"

Jeff paused. "That was it. Just like that. I left Satan and went to Jesus."

An Ex-Satanist Goes Church Hunting

As I have pondered the journeys of all those in this book, I wondered every time how the church would relate to these people from less-than-typical backgrounds. "I went to six different churches," Jeff told us. "No one knew how to relate to me."

I interrupted with a chuckle. "Jeff, most of us in churches really are not well equipped to relate to ex-satanists."

He smiled. "Well I'm glad someone did. In the seventh church, Harry and Jo Richardson came up to me after the service. They invited me to dinner in their home. It felt so comfortable being in a loving and Christian home."

Jeff felt comfortable as well telling them about his background.

"I just told them I had been a satanist for four years. Jo spoke up and said, 'You need someone to pray for you.' And when she prayed, I could sense this presence come out of me. And I could also tell that what was inside me was afraid; it left in fear."

Jeff ran to a mirror to look at himself. "I had not seen myself for years," he recalled. "Every time I looked in the mirror, I saw them, not me. For the first time in a long time, I saw 'me.' This joy came over me. I smiled so hard that it hurt."

We all needed to take a collective breath. The pleasant waitress came by to pick up the ticket and my payment, which included an extra tip to her for our prolonged stay in the restaurant.

"I learned," Jeff said slowly, "that Christlike love can reach anyone. It sure reached me. It is how I reach people in satanism and the occult today."

Jeff continued, "The key is unconditional love. The whole pagan society won't tolerate judgmental behavior. But they will find it hard to resist true Christlike love."

There it was again. That "love thing." How many times had we heard a similar testimony from those who told of their journeys? Can we Christians truly comprehend the power of the selfless type of love that we have through Christ? And are we willing to make the sacrifices necessary to demonstrate that love?

Reaching People Like Jeff

In light of Jeff's previous statements, I already anticipated Jeff's response to my question on how we can reach a satanist today. "It's love, man," he said, affirming my thoughts. "It's really just love."

He continued with another thought. "Christians do not need to fear the power of darkness. The media and some Word of Faith Christians have made this area seem out-of-bounds for Christians. You know, erroneous teachings that say if you walk into a certain place, you may become demonically influenced. I don't buy it. I believe the Word of God that says the gates of hell will not prevail against the church."

Jeff returned to his original point. "But the main thing is unconditional love. If we are willing to lay down our lives for people caught in darkness, we will see many in the occult become followers of Christ. That's the kind of witness that will make a difference. That's how you will reach them."

Nellie Jo and I did not want to leave. We felt like the conversation had really just begun. But a flight was waiting for us in Columbia, South Carolina. And as much as I would like to think that my airline would hold a flight for me since I'm a million-miler, I didn't want to take that chance.

We said our farewells to Jeff and Liz. They are such a radiant couple. I could easily see how God is using them. And as I got into the car, I said a prayer that God would honor their ministry and glorify himself through them. Somehow I sensed that the prayer had already been answered.

The day was still gray and dreary, but our spirits were bright and vibrant. Jeff and Liz Harshbarger are giving their lives for the sake of the gospel. They are touching many lives; I have no doubt they will touch many more.

As I saw the restaurant fade in the rearview mirror, I realized our *Unexpected Journey* was over. We had interviewed thirteen different people from twelve different belief systems. We had covered a territory that began in Salt Lake City, Utah, and ended in Augusta, Georgia. We had begun with former Mormons and concluded our travels with a former satanist.

Nellie Jo and I learned many things in this year of travels, research, and interviews. Some things we learned improved our knowledge of other faiths. But we learned more that changed our hearts and gave us a greater desire to be steady witnesses for Christ. These lessons also proved to be sources of great strength during Nellie Jo's battle with cancer. She found out about her malignancy just two weeks after this final interview. We are thankful that after two surgeries, four months of chemotherapy, and seven weeks of radiation therapy, she was doing well, and her prognosis is excellent.

In the last few pages of this book, I will share with you some of the lessons we learned. But first, let me thank you for joining us on *The Unexpected Journey*. I did not write this book with merely a desire to inform Christians about those of other faiths. Rather, my primary purpose was to see God use it to change hearts. So few Christians in America share their faith consistently. So few Christians are willing to lay down their lives for others. I pray that this book has been, above all, a heart-changing experience for you.

Now let's take one final look at these conversations and see what God has taught us that we might share with you.

CONCLUSION

AFTER THE UNEXPECTED JOURNEY

Nellie Jo decided to take a flight to Florida after our interviews for *The Unexpected Journey* concluded. She has an independent spirit. When she decides to go somewhere, she just takes off! On the plane she sat next to a young man in the army. Before the flight was over, she had shared the gospel more than one time with him.

On another flight she sat next to a successful businessman from California. Once again she was well received after she shared Christ with him. "Traveling with you on these interviews," Nellie Jo told me, "has given me a new boldness to share my faith. I have heard firsthand the depth of spiritual hunger. I am no longer hesitant to speak."

You see, our unexpected journey made an indelible impression on both of our lives. We entered into the world of miracles, and we have no desire to return to a world of mediocrity.

In the next few pages, I will share in condensed form the lessons we learned in our conversations with people who journeyed from other gods to faith in Christ.

Lesson 1: Know What You Believe

Most of the interviewees told us that they were amazed at the biblical ignorance they witnessed when they were not Christians. Several times we heard them say that they knew more about the Bible than Christians did. We cannot expect to defend the faith if we don't know what we believe. And we cannot know what we believe unless we spend time in the Bible.

Lesson 2: Know What They Believe

I really liked Mumin Muhammad's dream to establish departments or schools of apologetics in churches all across the world. We live in a highly pluralistic culture. Although we cannot expect every church member to have an in-depth knowledge of every belief system, we can train different members to reach out to a variety of persons in different belief systems.

Quite frankly, Christians often do more harm than good in our conversations with those of other faiths. We cannot expect to have their ears unless we have done our homework to find out as much as possible about what they believe. And that means we must listen to them, which is the next lesson.

Lesson 3: Listen to Them

I am a strong proponent of a verbal witness. But sometimes Christians are just too eager to talk and unwilling to listen. Several of *The Unexpected Journey* participants told us that they would have been much likelier to listen to Christians if the Christians would just listen to them as well.

Listening means we are willing to learn from others. Listening means we are not threatened in our own Christian beliefs by hearing what someone else believes. Listening means we really care for the person.

Lesson 4: Pray for Them

Some of the most "hopeless" persons became followers of Christ through the persistent prayers of Christians. How many churches actually set aside corporate prayer time to pray for those who do not have a personal relationship with Jesus Christ?

Lesson 5: Invite Them to Church

Guess who came to church? A Muslim, a witch, a Jehovah's Witness, two Mormons, a satanist, an atheist, an agnostic, a Buddhist, a New Ager, a Jew, a Hindu, and a Unitarian. In many cases these persons of other beliefs were invited to church and responded positively the first time they were invited.

I have done research in the past that shows that the vast majority of non-Christians will come to church if we invite them. What are we waiting for?

Lesson 6: Learn about Their Home Lives

Some of *The Unexpected Journey* participants shared with us some very sad stories of a difficult childhood and home life. If we listen with sensitivity to learn about others' childhood and youth, we can relate to them better.

Lesson 7: Get Them to Look Closely at Their Own Documents

Not all the belief systems we studied have their own doctrinal and historical documents. But many do. You have already heard the stories of the former Mormons and former Jehovah Witness who began doubting their religious systems when they examined their own documents thoroughly and openly. Of course, this approach presumes that the Christian has studied his or her belief system well.

Lesson 8: Encourage Them to Study the Bible Objectively

The Bible is God's Word. It will stand the test of any objections or doubt. The Bible is inspired by the Holy Spirit. God works to convict and convince through his Word. If a person of another faith system is so certain about his or her own beliefs, he or she should not fear studying what Christians believe with an open mind.

Lesson 9: Churches Must Be Prepared for a Pluralistic World

We heard it from Kathi, the former witch, and from Marcia, the former New Ager: they both attended churches for weeks and never heard the gospel presented. This situation is a travesty in the American church. Pastors and other church leaders must realize that each week someone may be attending who is spiritually dying. The gospel is their only hope.

The church also must be ready to disciple persons who have become Christians out of other belief systems. Countless times we heard in our interviews that the churches did not know what to do with these "strange" people once they became followers of Christ.

Lesson 10: Christians Cannot Be Intimidated by Other Beliefs

Would you be intimidated to share Christ with a witch? I am sure I would have had my own fear factor prior to *The Unexpected Journey*. But then I heard Kathi Sharpe's life story of incredible struggles. I learned the lesson that she was deeply hurting on the inside, hoping and waiting for someone to show love and compassion.

Would you be intimidated to share Christ with a satanist? Jeff Harshbarger taught me that his life's path included many personal difficulties. If Christians had taken the time to get to know him, perhaps they would have had more compassion and less fear.

Christians have nothing to fear. The gates of hell will not prevail against us. We have nothing to fear, but in Christ's name, we have much to offer.

Lesson 11: Share Your Faith Regularly

In the course of a year, only one person becomes a Christian in America for every 85 church members. Christians have become spiritually lazy and disobedient. Telling others the good news of Jesus Christ is not optional for any Christian. It is not something left to the pastors and ministers we sometimes treat like hired hands. It is the calling and the mandate of every Christian.

Lesson 12: Live Like a Christian

Before "WWJD" (What would Jesus do?) became a popular slogan among Christians, the question was one of my favorites. I came across it when I read Charles Sheldon's book *In His Steps* more than twenty years ago.

I believe without a doubt, after listening to these twelve extraordinary stories, that persons of other faiths would be strongly drawn to Christians if we just acted like Christians should act. Wouldn't it be a different world if every Christian preceded each decision and conversation by asking what Jesus would do?

Lesson 13: Be Willing to Invest Time with Non-Christians

For many Christians, witnessing is a one-time verbal shot. But most of those with whom we spoke needed someone who would be willing to invest time with them. Christ spent time with people even though his recorded earthly ministry was only about three years. Will Christians today be willing to develop long and sacrificial relationships with those who are not followers of Christ? Such an act is a true act of love, our final but most important lesson.

Lesson 14: Love People with Christ's Unconditional Love

Repeatedly we heard it in our conversations. The theme permeated almost the entirety of this project. The message was inescapable: non-Christians are drawn to those who demonstrate Christlike love. What exactly does Christlike love look like? Listen to the direct quotes from *The Unexpected Journey*.

> "She was so nonjudgmental. I never pictured Christians to be that way."

> "He refused to stop praying for me, even when I cursed him and threw things at him."

> "She showed up at our house with food in a time of great need."

> "They were willing to let their home be my home. They always had a meal for me, and they would do anything for me."

> "He accepted me when everybody else looked at my weird dress and appearance and rejected me."

> "I know I bugged her to death with all the questions I had, but she listened and responded with compassion and

concern. That continued for over fourteen months. Can you imagine someone investing that much time in me?"

"I always thought love had to be earned. But then he told me that Jesus loved me unconditionally. I was speechless."

I could repeat dozens of quotes such as those above. But the picture painted is clear. We who are Christians can win many to Christ if we just demonstrate the love that Christ commanded us to show. The hurting world waits for people just like that.

An Unexpected Journey Farewell

This *Unexpected Journey* is complete. The keyboard is about to go silent for a season. But thirteen people have touched Nellie Jo's and my life forever.

The title of this book, *The Unexpected Journey*, was supposed to reflect the surprising ways Christ revealed himself to those to whom we spoke. But at the end of the day, the title also portrays the story of Nellie Jo and me.

We started *The Unexpected Journey* thinking that we would be dispassionate reporters chronicling others' stories. How wrong we were! We too were surprised. We were amazed. And we were touched by the love of Christ so evident in each of these lives.

Thank you again Rauni, Dennis, Steve, Ravi, Mrs. J., Paul, Mia, Kathi, Helena, Karan, Marcia, Mumin, and Jeff. I hope I will get to see you again. But if I do not, I know one thing for certain. I *will* see you at that great reunion that awaits all of us who have placed our trust in Christ. To God be the glory!

QUESTIONS FOR REFLECTION AND DISCUSSION

Chapter 1: Mormonism

1. Why are people often attracted to Mormonism?

2. What are some key reasons that those in the Mormon Church find it difficult to leave their beliefs and their church?

3. What are some steps a Christian can take to be more effective in reaching out to Mormons?

Chapter 2: Judaism

1. What are the similarities between the Jewish faith and the Christian faith? What are the differences?

2. Why do many Jews resist Christians who tell them they need to convert to Christianity?

3. What are some steps a Christian can take to be more effective in reaching out to Jews?

Chapter 3: Hinduism

1. How do the concepts of karma and reincarnation affect the lives of Hindus?

2. How is Hinduism a religion of works, and how do the ultimate goals of Hinduism and Christianity compare and contrast?

3. What are some steps a Christian can take to be more effective in reaching out to Hindus?

Chapter 4: Atheism

1. Why are many atheists intensely opposed to Christians and Christianity?

2. What is the role of apologetics for the Christian in his or her interaction with atheists?

3. What are some steps a Christian can take to be more effective in reaching out to atheists?

Chapter 5: Jehovah's Witnesses

1. What features do Christianity and Jehovah's Witnesses have in common? What are the key differences?

2. Why are many people attracted to the beliefs of Jehovah's Witnesses?

3. What are some steps a Christian can take to be more effective in reaching out to Jehovah's Witnesses?

Chapter 6: Agnosticism

1. Why are all agnostics not alike in their beliefs?

2. What life events could possibly influence people toward becoming agnostic in their beliefs?

3. What are some steps a Christian can take to be more effective in reaching out to agnostics?

Chapter 7: Wiccan

1. Why might someone choose to become a witch or to practice other pagan beliefs?

2. What misconceptions about witches are common today?

3. What are some steps a Christian can take to be more effective in reaching out to witches and other pagans?

Chapter 8: Buddhism

1. How is Buddhism significantly different than Christianity?

2. What is the ultimate hope of a Buddhist?

3. What are some steps a Christian can take to be more effective in reaching out to Buddhists?

Chapter 9: Unitarianism

1. What are some unique aspects of Unitarianism?

2. Why can it be said that many people today are Unitarians even if they are not formally associated with a Unitarian congregation?

3. What are some steps a Christian can take to be more effective in reaching out to Unitarians?

Chapter 10: New Ageism

1. Why is the New Age Movement difficult to define? How would you define it?

2. Why would someone be drawn to New Age beliefs?

3. What are some steps a Christian can take to be more effective in reaching out to people in the New Age Movement? Do you know anyone in this category for whom you could be praying?

Chapter 11: Islam

1. What are some similarities between Christianity and Islam? What are major differences?

2. What are some unique beliefs of Black Muslims within the larger Islamic community?

3. What are some steps a Christian can take to be more effective in reaching out to Muslims?

Chapter 12: Satanism

1. What are some of the different and even contradicting beliefs among those who called themselves satanists?

2. Why are many Christians reluctant to involve themselves with people in satanism and other occultist beliefs? Is this reluctance justified?

3. What are some steps a Christian can take to be more effective in reaching out to satanists and others in the occult?